Drama
for people with special needs

Ann Cattanach

Second edition

A&C Black · London
Drama Publishers · New York

Second edition 1996
First published 1992
A&C Black (Publishers) Limited
35 Bedford Row, London WCIR 4JH

ISBN 0–7136–4384–6

Published simultaneously in the U.S.A. by
Drama Publishers, 260 Fifth Avenue,
New York, New York 10001.

ISBN 0–89676–144–4

CIP catalogue records for this book
are available from the British Library
and the Library of Congress.

Cover photographs by Claire Godfrey, reproduced
by kind permission of the Strathcona Theatre Company

Typeset in 10½ on 12 pt Sabon by Florencetype Limited,
Stoodleigh, Devon
and printed in Great Britain by Redwood Books, Trowbridge, Wilts

Contents

1

Drama for helping and healing

AIM OF THE BOOK

The aim of this book is to explore the use of drama as a means of helping and healing for those people who have special needs. The emphasis of the book is on practical methods of dramatic exploration which can be shared with groups and individuals. It is important to know what is meant by 'dramatic exploration' in the context of helping and healing so that the boundaries of the work can be established.

DRAMATIC EXPLORATIONS

This way of exploring ourselves and our experiences through drama is not new, it has been an essential part of human development from earliest times. It is one of the most powerful ways we define ourselves and our relations to others.

Huizinga (1949) writes:

The spirit of playful competition is, as a social impulse, older than culture and pervades all life like a veritable ferment. Ritual grew up in sacred play; poetry was born in play and nourished on play; music and dancing were pure play . . . We have to conclude therefore that civilisation is in its earliest phases played. It does not come from play like a babe detaching itself from the womb, it arises in and as play and never leaves it.

This concept of the centrality of play and drama in our cultural life is an extension of the natural play of children who use spontaneous dramatic enactments from an early age to experiment and make sense of their experience.

1

We can use drama in the same playful way as a medium in which to give some creative structure to experience. We can experiment with creative solutions to problems by making a fictitious dramatic world in which we can play with an infinite variety of choices with the great advantage that we do not have to live with the solutions we make.

In this fictitious world of our own making, we can experiment with roles, situations and ways of being which we might never want to experience in reality but still want to explore in the safety of fiction.

One of the most important concepts in the arts is this idea of aesthetic illusion.

AESTHETIC ILLUSION

When we work with drama in the group or individually as we use drama forms like improvisation, stories, games, etc., we create a symbolic or metaphoric world where the power to change or reconstruct events belongs to the group or individual. We are making acts of representation through which we can interpret or reinterpret our own or others' experiences in dramatic form.

As we make these actions in drama, we experience the illusional element of the drama process and this can make playing safer for the group.

Susan Langer (1953) in her book *Feeling and Form* describes aesthetic illusion in the arts as an otherness from reality, a detachment from actuality. She states that all forms of art are abstracted forms in a context of illusion.

This means we can examine our illusional world free from the constraints of real circumstances. There are no chance accidents or irrelevancies to obscure the logic of the illusional world so we can develop new meanings for ourselves uncluttered by the constraints of our own reality. We can escape from being the victims of our own circumstances. Jane aged 5, for example, had been sexually abused by her cousin of 14. In her play she devised a monster whom she could control. She made up stories about this monster and a little girl who defeated him. We acted the stories together, she felt powerful and through controlling the monster she learnt strategies of dealing with powerful people who control and bully. She also became the monster and through acting this role she began to experience the whole dynamic of the relationship between her monster and child. All this was done through dramatic enactments.

Robert Rauschenberg (1981), the artist, says of his work that his painting relates to both art and life. Neither can be made. He tries to act in the gap between the two.

It is in this gap between art and life, in a sort of timeless space, that we can experiment with ways of being which can help and heal both the individual and the group.

PLAYFULNESS

When Jane created her monster and made up stories about him she told me she was 'just playing'. She found this notion very important as she discovered she could be in charge of her own creation, and structure the stories and drama for herself choosing the kind of play that was important for her, stopping and starting her stories as she chose. But most of all, she was playing, safe from real monsters and able in her play always to win and scrunch the monster to pieces.

Play and culture

Huizinga (1949) considered playfulness an important feature of our cultural life. He suggested that in play there was something 'at play' which transcended the immediate needs of life and imparted meaning to the action. It was a stepping out of 'real' life into a temporary sphere of activity. At the same time there was an intensity and absorption in play. Play was also distinct from ordinary life both as to its locality and duration. There were limits to play; it began and then it was over. Huizinga also suggested that play assumed a fixed form as a cultural phenomenon. Once played it endured as a new found creation of the mind retained by the memory. It was transmitted, it became tradition.

This experience of tradition is often to be found in drama groups. Once a story or scene is made it is often repeated at subsequent meetings and talked about as part of the mythology of the group. In this way the group develops its own cultural identity.

For example, one group of adolescent boys insisted on starting every session with the game of one in the middle guessing which person in the group was holding a marble as it was passed round from hand to hand. They became very skilled at the game and developed new rules and variations each week. These boys were considered failures by their teachers at school so it was important for them to have a skill which they could show to an adult who was impressed by their dexterity. They showed they could be consistently good at something the adult valued. This formed a bond between members of the group and the bond was about valuing each other's skills. Being good at something, getting better and being praised by an adult. Rare indeed!

When describing play as a cultural phenomenon, Huizinga stated that all play had rules and the rules determined what 'held' in the temporary world circumscribed by play. If the rules of play were broken it robbed play of its illusion. Even very young children are clear about this rule. How often do we hear a child stop and say, 'I'm not playing,' once the rules are broken. So play has cultural value because:

1 it stands outside 'ordinary' life,
2 it absorbs the player utterly and intensely,
3 it is safe – we can create fictional worlds free from the constraints of 'ordinary' life,
4 the safety of play also lies in the rules that boundary the process.

Huizinga examined play as a cultural phenomenon, Kliphuis (1975) considered that playfulness had psychological relevance.

The psychological relevance of 'playfulness'
Kliphuis emphasised the protective effect of the playful element. Because it is 'play' and not real life the player is to some degree protected from feelings of guilt and anxiety which would otherwise prevent him from expressing feelings and fulfilling needs.

Kliphuis was examining the work of the Creative Therapist and he suggested that the structure present in art forms could be used by the therapist to help clients expose their own creativity in safety.

In working with groups who have special needs, one of the most important functions of the leader is to offer drama forms and techniques which can best express the ideas and feelings of the group but which will also keep the group safe and comfortable.

For example, Mary was a 24 year old woman who frequently responded to stress by inflicting injuries on her arms. Mary wanted to explore this need but couldn't find a way to express it. In the group we experimented with various drama forms but Mary found the experience too painfully real. Then with a friend she wrote a scene for two players about a girl, not herself, who harmed herself. The technique of writing and then performing the scene gave Mary enough distance from herself to take pride in her creative abilities.

The scene was acted in the group many times. There were speaking parts for an audience. Mary asked members of the group to play the girl in her scene and she and others took roles as the audience. Mary took great pleasure in hearing what she had written being performed and as the material became familiar the intensity of Mary's emotion about the subject matter diminished. She became more at ease with herself and especially proud of her ability to write dramatic material.

PLAY AS A DEVELOPMENTAL PROCESS

Sue Jennings (1990) describes the play of children evolving through three developmental stages from early infant experiences to the complex dramatic play of the young child. These three stages are: embodiment play, projective play and role play.

Embodiment play

Embodiment play includes those pre-play explorations of the world through the senses as the infant touches, tastes, sees and experiences the immediate sensory world. This starts at a very early age before the child begins to walk and when that happens the child can then experiment with a much wider environment. These marvellous initial sensory experiences lay the foundation of our sense of self and our pleasure in the physical world. Many children and indeed adults find enjoyment and a renewed sense of self through regressing to these early stages of play. For many of us who, for whatever reasons, missed out on much of this kind of play, to recreate a different infanthood is one of the pleasures of drama work.

Projective play

Projective play develops as the child begins to explore the world of objects and toys external to herself and symbolic play begins.

Play with objects develops from simple action patterns when the infant grasps an attractive object and develops through the exploration and investigation of objects to sequences of more complex play. In these explorations the child learns that toys and objects can replicate things in the real world. From explorations of objects which go together such as toy knife, fork, spoon, plate, to sequences which go together such as eating an imaginary dinner from toy plates. In the next stage the infant invents objects which are not present and then transforms objects so that one object represents another: thus a chair becomes a car, the saucepan a crown. The child then plays in the 'as if' mode: 'Let's play as if the chair were a car.'

Vygotsky (1933) described the process when a child plays with a stick and calls that stick a horse and uses the stick as a horse in play. The child then learns the meaning of horse apart from the real animal. When the child severs the meaning of horse from the real animal he learns to 'think' horse. The stick and the play with the stick as a horse are pivots to recall the absent object. Through this the child learns that every object has a meaning. Vygotsky called this reality perception, that we experience the world as having sense and meaning.

Role play

Children begin 'let's pretend' play with activities in which the role taken is one of self-representation, then through experiments with toys and other children they eventually learn to pretend to be somebody else. Piaget (1962) stated that this was not imitation because the child does more than copy the behaviour of others so that while still being himself he identifies completely with others. This is the paradox of role-taking in play.

As children learn to play other people then they begin to involve themselves in role play with other children and adults. By four years of age children can adapt and combine their role play with the make-believe play of other children.

DRAMA AS A GROUP PROCESS

Drama has its own unique characteristics but when a group participate in drama we must also remember that the negotiations and interactions which are part of any group can also be observed in the drama group.

As in all groups the process evolves and develops through the interactions of group members and leader as the culture of the group emerges. There is a continuous dynamic present in the group as relationships develop, conflict, move forward or stand still. When change occurs there is a disturbance in the tension of the group until the change has been absorbed.

The individual in the group is confronted with the emotions she feels about her place and role in the group, her feelings for the group leader and how she feels the creative task of the group is progressing.

In drama for helping and healing, the drama process is the central focus of the group. The medium of drama is used in a structured way to activate the group although the use made of drama and the use made of the structure of the group are ultimately for the benefit of the emotional development of each individual in the group.

In the drama group all these processes function continuously and actively while the group exist. There is the emotional and internal process of each group member, the creative development of each individual, the group dynamic process in the group and the creative development of the group.

What we explore in group drama within the drama is dramatic structure and dramatic role. Sue Jennings (1986) writes that in the drama group we explore predictable structures that have led to unhelpful behaviour and try to find some creative alternatives, we re-develop appropriate roles through practice and remodelling and develop new roles that are appropriate to different situations. We create new possibilities from our experiences of playing scenes and discover new ways of connecting internalised responses with external behaviour and vice versa.

THE ROLE OF THE GROUP LEADER

The leader has a variety of functions for the group. She is the technical expert on drama skills and group process. She has the technical knowledge of how drama can be effectively presented and understands the restrictions of the medium. This information can be made known to the group as members require it. The leader understands and can comment on phases in the drama process and help when group members get stuck. She also has the skill to observe and comment upon the interactions of the group and finally the leader can help group members to get in touch with their creative imagination and through the drama process use this imagination to enhance the individual's sense of well-being.

It is important that the leader understands the need for a clear structure in a drama session to help the group through the process of making a piece of drama. This structure should be balanced by the ability of the leader to create a mood and environment which can stimulate the work.

This is a delicate balance to achieve. Too much structure, no stimulation, means no interaction between group and leader, just going through the motions. Too much stimulation and no clear structure means high levels of anxiety and a desire by the group to discharge tension as quickly as possible so that response is fight or flight and the work is set aside.

I worked with a small group of angry 13 year old boys. We met once a week. This week they want to be clowns. They all agree to this theme. There is an immediate eruption of 'clowning'. When all is quiet we talk of the clowns we have seen. What they do, how they look, their personalities. We look at pictures. I advise on make-up. Then we discuss what kind of drama we want to make. We decide on a circus act. It will be mime with vocal sound to express the moods of the clowns. We work on these skills. We sort out clothes and I show how to apply the make-up. They look at themselves in the mirror with the clowns' clothes and faces. They try out their voices and clown personalities looking in the mirror. They try out their circus act. Then again and again. Then for the last time. They take off their make-up and costumes and relax and define what has happened in the group.

It is important for the leader to make it safe for the group to be creative so that the drama process can be worked through to a satisfactory resolution. As the group start to function, the leader is the unifying force. Members of the group initially relate to each other through their common relationship with the leader.

The leader is responsible initially for the negotiation and

establishment of the codes of behaviour which will help and guide the interaction of the group. The creative process in drama should be made clear to the group: how the process works and what drama forms can express. The leader works in the 'here and now' of the creative process. Conflicts erupt and resolutions are made in the process of making drama. It is important for the leader to be able to comment on the creative process. She must find methods of working which will achieve some self affirmation for members of the group through their creative efforts. As personal conflicts arise in solving creative problems the leader comments on these conflicts as they affect the drama process.

To develop the example of the group working on clowns. At the beginning of the session, when the theme of clowns is discussed there is an immediate explosion of 'clowning'. This is the normal beginning for this group. We have recognised that beginning is difficult and creates anxiety. We either make a warm-up game to use the surplus energy or, as in this case, use our theme in a loud, noisy way to feel more comfortable with the material. I bring the group to a more relaxed state with a quick physical warm-up, then we sit to talk and explore our theme. One boy is depressed. Can he use his mood in the play? Yes, he will be a sad clown. Yes, but why is the clown sad? We decide it is watching the behaviour of the other clowns that makes him so sad. So he can now develop his role as observer of the other clowns with occasional bursts of loud clownish howls. He enjoys this passive role with active bursts.

We sort out clothes and make-up – lots of fighting and arguments but all resolved in who wears what. The group begins to sort out the clown acts. We work together on the development of activities and the personal characteristics of each clown. An argument begins over how to work out a balancing trick. Two boys get angry and begin to fight. The group have previously agreed that I can referee arguments and fighting should be minimal. The fight disrupts the drama. We stop the fight and work out why it happened.

With this group I used process comments in the sequence suggested by Yalom (1975) in his book *The Theory and Practice of Group Psychotherapy*. Firstly here is what your behaviour is like. Through feedback from others in the group and self observation we may learn about our behaviour. Secondly, here is how your behaviour makes others feel. We learn to see ourselves as others experience us. Thirdly, here is how our behaviour influences the opinion others have of us. We discover that others find our behaviour amusing, irritating or perhaps frightening. Finally, here is how our behaviour influences our opinion of ourselves. This is understood by building on the information gathered from the first three steps.

In the drama group, this kind of commentary is related to the way an individual is working in the group during the drama process. The level of comment is as much as a group can accept or absorb. The fighting pair is with a group which have been working for some time so I can ask other members how they feel about solving problems by fighting. Some express irritation that the fighting stopped the drama so we agree to go on with the drama and solve the problem of the balancing trick by working on it a little longer. The work begins again.

The clowns present their acts. We do it again and again until we feel satisfied. Then we reflect on what we have achieved. The discussion is about the feelings experienced when we see our faces in all that make-up. How you pick up the personality of the clown by the way we see our faces. We talk about masks. We decide to work with masks the next week.

We decide to finish with a game we all like. Sometimes it happens like that, other times we get part way through the process then anger or anxiety overwhelms creativity and it's a slow haul through to get back to the drama.

Otto Rank (1932/1975) in his book *Art and Artist* suggested that the neurotic person is a failed artist. That the neurotic concentrates the whole personality on every detail of experience and as this is practically impossible and psychically painful he protects himself by powerful inner restraints, cutting off from the world and experience. Faced with the proposition 'All or Nothing', he chooses nothing. Rank suggests that the artist chooses the constructive middle way. He avoids the loss of himself in life not by staying negative but by living himself out in creative work. The leader of the drama group is trying to persuade the group to try the artist's way.

DRAMA WORK IN THE GROUP

There are many kinds of drama which can be developed with a group and a specific focus will emerge defined by the needs of the group.

Sue Jennings identified models of practice in dramatherapy which state the prime focus of the therapy and the structure which enables it to take place. Firstly the Creative-Expressive model where the focus is on developing the healthy aspects of people. The drama structures used stimulate the imagination and develop creative energy in people. Secondly the Tasks and Skills model which uses drama as a way of practising the skills we need in everyday life, for example, role-playing social situations that are unfamiliar. Thirdly the Psychotherapeutic model where the focus is on insight and change through the use of the methodology of a psychotherapy group. In this model drama will be used to highlight psychotherapeutic processes working with transferences, introjection and projection to effect change and modify behaviour. These models of practice are for the use of drama as therapy but some models can be effective with drama for helping and healing for people with special needs.

I would suggest three models of practice in offering drama for special needs: Creative-Expressive, Tasks and Skills and Self Advocacy.

Creative-Expressive model
This is a very important model of drama for special needs. The focus is on the healthy aspects of people and the stimulus of the work is to help individuals and the group to discover their own creative potential in drama.

There is much exploration through the forms of play and improvised drama in this model with an emphasis on communication both verbal and non-verbal. There is a need to make communication with other members of the group to play in this way and social skills develop through playing together. The development of this work is through the developmental stages of play from embodiment play to projected and symbolic play to role play.

This way of working builds up the confidence of the individual and the nurturing power of the group and can enhance self esteem for people who have limited experience of drama. It is always important to begin within the capacities of the group so skills develop at an appropriate pace.

Skill in creative-expressive play does not rely on the ability to express complex roles and can be very successful with limited or no verbal communication. However, as the group gain confidence and skills then role playing can develop and theatre ideas can be explored if members wish to develop this form. Many groups really enjoy the experience of creative play, given the opportunity in the group to rediscover the childhood freedom of 'let's pretend'. Through the use of games and other forms of play the group begin to build imaginative ideas into dramatic form.

I worked in this mode with a small group of young women who had been sexually abused in childhood. They didn't want to explore their past experience of abuse, they wanted to find out about drama. We used a lot of movement and voice work in ways that were individual experiences shared with the whole group but no small-group work which threatened their newly discovered autonomy over their own bodies. From this work we developed play and improvisation where they began to enjoy sharing ideas with each other in ways which were not always open to them as young children. They began to re-enact a more open and playful childhood free from power-dominated communication which had been their earlier experience. There were still times of mistrust in the group and suspicion of the motives of others but much of this was resolved and pleasure and pride in their imaginative capacities were strongly felt.

Another group of profoundly disabled young children used simple movement and any sounds they could make to develop communication with helpers and other children in the group. The sounds they made were pre-verbal babbling but used in quite complex and rhythmic ways rather like singing a round. Individual pleasure in engaging with others and offering a movement or sound which was taken up and expanded by the others developed the capacity of the group and though no words were used the communication was complex. The movement involved rocking and rolling along the floor or being gently pushed and rocked. Eventually we were able to combine some of the movement and sounds together in simple communication sequences.

Tasks and Skills model

This kind of drama group can involve general social skills, learning appropriate social interaction through the use of drama or perhaps taking a particular task such as learning about body boundaries for children who have been sexually abused.

With people from a particular ethnic group it can be an exciting way of learning about the cultural heritage and present values of the group.

Sometimes a group can be formed to share experiences of a particular difficulty such as diabetes, and drama can be a powerful way of learning about the illness as well as sharing some of the feelings illness engenders.

I worked with a group of diabetic adolescents which met at the hospital once a month. We began a session with drama methods using improvisation to build a scene. The theme was chosen by the group. The scene was in a hospital where a diabetic adolescent and her mother came to see the consultant. I played the mother, the nurse/counsellor who worked with the group was the adolescent. The members of the group were consultants, nurses, receptionists. In the role play I was at my wit's end with my daughter who wouldn't do the tasks required to keep her condition stable. She was a very disaffected adolescent. The consultant told her very firmly what the consequences of this behaviour might be. I asked a lot of questions about the illness and what my daughter must do. I received clear answers to all my questions. As the role play progressed the communication became clear and firm and my daughter and I got a strong message about the illness and the consequences of not understanding or caring about the condition.

At the end of the role play the group said how much they enjoyed dishing out the advice for a change instead of just receiving it. At the same time giving the information had clarified the reasons for some of the tedious tasks needed to keep the illness in check. I asked questions and was given information by the group, who clearly knew more about diabetes than I did. At other times they were also able to express the powerlessness they felt with the constant monitoring required and how it can overwhelm and engulf and absorb so much of life especially for an adolescent. It is hard to be so controlled at a time in life when you want to rebel and the anxiety of parents weigh even more heavily upon you because of your condition.

Another group of young children tackled the difficulties of playground bullying through making up scenes and devising ways of avoiding trouble for themselves at playtime. There had been a lot of difficult behaviour in the playground at school where there were many corners and buildings which made it difficult for adults to see what was happening. The children in the group were aged about 6. They worked together playing out the kind of bullying they had observed or experienced at first hand. This group proved to be one of the most honest and direct. They communicated their behaviour to each other and how it made them feel. They devised clever strategies to cope with the 'bossy' people and challenged the control of such children in their own group. Their skill would have done credit to a professional adult negotiator. They also began to recognise that their feelings mattered, and they didn't have to endure hurt and humiliation in silence. The group played continuously, only talking about the play for a short time at the end. All the negotiating was achieved in the play and learning took place 'on the hoof' as it were, as they played over and over to make sense of their situation.

Self Advocacy model

If people with special needs identify themselves and wish to form a group of like-minded people then they may choose in the group to explore self advocacy to describe the oppression they feel or explore ways of validating their experience to the community at large.

There are many theatre and drama forms which can be used to present self advocacy, from research and presentation of a particular theme which is a matter of agreed concern in the group to exploration of theatre forms like those presented in the concepts of Augusto Boal (1979) in what he defined as the *Theatre of the Oppressed*.

His work explores the frontiers between theatre, drama and psychotherapy. He defined his theatre methods as a way to transform reality. He states that when the oppressed produce their own images of their own oppression they create a work of art. These images come out of real life but are aesthetically transubstantiated to create a work of art. In this way the oppressed belong in two different worlds and each of the worlds is autonomous: the world of reality and the world of its image which they themselves have made. The world of the image presents the oppressions in transubstantiated form, and once in this fictive world its coherence must be maintained. When the work of the created image is being explored, no reference is made back to the world which generated the image. Each of the two worlds has its own organic existence.

Boal defined the process as:

beginning with our own reality which contains oppression;

the oppression is defined;

we transform the oppression into an image or a fiction (which is real in so far as it is an image);

we ask, 'What do we want to change?'

we transform the image which we have created and through using the image and exploring its form dramatically the possibilities for change can be revealed;

we return to reality and transform it.

Boal developed a variety of techniques of the *Theatre of the Oppressed*, in particular Forum Theatre where actors perform a play which they have devised in response to a community's oppression. The actors are led by the 'Joker' who explains the rules of the game to the spectators, then the actors begin to do the play again. This time the spectators can tell the actors to stop whenever they see a better way for the actor to follow. The spectator can then replace the character and play an alternative action. In this way Boal breaks down the split between actor and spectator and uses the theatre as a rehearsal for social change. In this form of theatre the spectator delegates no power to the actor to act or think in his place, he himself can assume the role, change the dramatic action, try out solutions, discuss plans for change and in that way train himself for real action.

The group of diabetic adolescents began to play the oppression they felt about their condition and the control it assumed over their lives. From that workshop they produced a television script, giving information about the pressures of being an adolescent and also about being diabetic. This was made into a video which won a competition. The video was to be used as information about being diabetic so they became advocates for other adolescent diabetics. They had learnt communication skills and were more able to talk about their needs in their treatment programme.

Two women explored the oppression of power relationships which became sado-masochistic. They explored this way of

being and made fictional images from their experience of relationships in their own lives. Through their intense exploration
of the images they made, they saw the possibilities for change
and played them in their fictive world.

These two examples explore some of the ideas of Boal.
Companies of actors who work in the community use Forum
Theatre as a way to help groups find their own voice.

The Rainbow of Desire

Boal has further developed his ideas about personal oppression
in his book *The Rainbow of Desire* (1985). He calls this the
Boal method of theatre and therapy and explores the use of
theatre as a therapeutic tool for those who are oppressed not
only by external forces but by internalised 'cops in the head'.
He suggests that the 'cops' are in our heads but that their
'headquarters and barracks' are on the outside. The aim is to
discover a way to dislodge them.

Here Boal locates the politics of the individual. He explores
the potential of theatre to liberate the individual from
oppressions such as fear, emptiness and the difficulties of
communicating with others.

He suggests that individuals cannot be changed by a voiding
of desires but that desires can be clarified and dynamised. This
is Boal's definition of catharsis: a release of desires which
societal constrictions (such as family, school or work) have
imprisoned.

The basic techniques for this are incorporated in Image
Theatre. It begins with an initial improvisation that looks into
somebody's real-life experience of internalised oppression. The
improvisation is directed by the protagonist who plays him/
herself.

It is then used as the basis for a more comprehensive exploration. Images of the characters in the story – seen or unseen
in the improvisation, but detected – are made and offered by
both the protagonist who created the improvisation and the
larger group of spectators present.

The images are then brought to life in a variety of ways and
the results observed objectively.

Objective and subjective commentaries are then invited from
the spectators and must be clearly in one of these categories.
These multiple readings are often wildly at odds with each
other. The observations are collated, discussed and relayed

back to the protagonist. It is up to the protagonist to make of them what he or she will.

Boal suggests that individuals can be the directors of their own therapeutic processes, not just passive recipients, and he emphasises that the ideas and techniques should be adapted to the participants, not the participants to the ideas.

It is suggested that *The Rainbow of Desire* method is accessible to any group with sufficient duration, stability and preparation time for the work but the criteria for such a group are not defined.

The techniques of Image Theatre could help a group to explore the interface between personal and external oppressions in a most productive way provided that boundaries of safety and care were made and maintained so the process was life-enhancing. There are dangers in personal therapeutic explorations in a group if there are poor ground rules and boundaries are not made clear.

The role of director is crucial in these forms of exploration and there must be a level of trust and confidentiality established within the group before such personal drama can be developed.

Boal does not appear to describe any techniques of closure for these group explorations and no follow-up evaluations of his methods are known to have taken place. This means that participants have to take responsibility for themselves and for fellow group members if the safety of the group is to be maintained.

2

Drama methods

DRAMA MEDIA FOR GROUPS AND INDIVIDUALS

When a group explore themes in drama they try to find resolutions using symbolic forms. The symbolic forms are defined through the use of media. The media are determined by the shape the explorations take and this shape in turn helps the group learn about the nature of the media and the nature of the exploration.

The main media for dramatic exploration are: body, movement, voice, language, objects, space and time. In drama we use our own self as medium in the way we do in everyday behaviour but changed and transformed by dramatic structure. In drama we explore ideas by showing behaviour and social action but represented symbolically. Even reproduction of actual events becomes transformed through the way it is shown and the choice of what is shown.

Drama has a beginning, then it is over, it takes place in time and space. The dramatic statements we make exist in the act of making them, then they are over. When the action stops the statement fades. The ephemeral nature of drama is a powerful force for healing. The images and enactments we have created are over but their impact goes on working as we internalise and make sense of what we have created. That is the healing force: sharing our creativity, the images we have made and the impact of those images on our inner and outer life.

18

SKILLS IN DRAMA

Skill in the use of the media is very important for the artistic endeavours of the group and the sense of well-being and empowerment of all the group members. It is patronising to have low expectations of the level of skill in a group. It is the job of the leader to help the group members develop enough skills to be able to explore themes that are important for the group. The leader should be able to give individuals and the group confidence in their ability to portray ideas, feelings and events dramatically.

People with special needs have often developed a high degree of skill in a specific area which can be harnessed in drama. For example, abused children from violent backgrounds are often described as 'hypervigilant', forever watching to ward off the blows. In drama this capacity to observe detail can be used in play, the skill praised. Being extra-observant in order to be creative instead of through fear is a transformation in itself and in this way can begin a healing process for children.

So how does the group leader begin to help develop drama skills with groups who have done little drama and whose special needs must be considered so the group feels safe and contained? One way to start this process is to begin at the beginning by exploring drama and play as a developmental process.

DRAMA AND PLAY AS A DEVELOPMENTAL PROCESS

A way to start to empower a group is to work through the medium of play following the developmental processes in the way children learn to play. This creates a cultural life for the group. This process evolves through three stages: embodiment play, projective play and role play. We must remember that play is at the root of artistic expression and any drama process requires the participants to embody, project and enact creative material, that is what drama and acting are about. Using the developmental model for drama only separates out a process that is basic to all drama and theatre forms.

Remembering childhood play
For those group members fortunate enough to have played happily in childhood it is a rewarding experience to go back

and be creative as in their childhood although the content of the play in drama would be age appropriate. For those in the group who have not experienced this kind of play, it can be the awakening of a creative fluidity and a reworking of past experience in a happier form. To be given permission to play in a group and enjoy that experience is the beginning of a creative life and sets up rituals which keep the group safe.

Some groups with special needs, for example those with learning difficulties or physical immobilities, can play as appropriate for their developmental or physical level but the ingenuity of the leader can offer creative alternatives through choices of media. For those adults and children who have lost the ability to be creative, then play is the safe way to explore their possibilities.

EMBODIMENT PLAY

This is one way to get in touch with sensory awareness and sensory memory and perhaps to recall early infant experiences of play. The aim of this kind of play is to sensitise the body; this is the beginning of learning the languages of drama and theatre. Boal (1979) states that the language of the theatre consists of verbal language, but as important are the language of body, image and symbol.

Relaxation and body awareness

SUGGESTION

Find your own private space.

Relax, lying on your back.

Close your eyes and imagine you are a creature in the prehistoric past.

You are a formless creature, alive because you are breathing.

You have been safe and warm floating in soft mud for a million years.

All you have done is breathe and float and breathe and float.

As you imagine being that creature, lying, floating, encased in soft mud, your body feels so relaxed that movement is impossible.

You feel soft and warm and safe.

Breathe and feel the warm mud – and you float and breathe and float.

(Allow 3 minutes talking in this way where appropriate for the group.)

Then gradually you know that for some powerful reason you have to move and leave the safety of the enveloping mud, in which you have lived for so many centuries.

You must leave the mud and crawl to dry land.

You must leave, crawl out of the mud to sit on the dry land.

How do you begin to stir and move having simply been cushioned by the mud?

How do you begin to move a body which has never moved before?

But you feel inside that you must move.

But how?

How do you begin to move from lying on your back to crawl and finally sit and look around?

(The leader talks with the group to encourage them to move from their relaxed state of floating into rolling over and crawling to the edge of the mud. This takes about five minutes before the group responds.)

This metaphor is a powerful way to get in touch with the enormous task of the young child from birth to walking or perhaps the more primitive struggle to be a human who moves. The symbolic evolutionary struggle.

These images are powerful for those with special needs who continually struggle with the body.

SUGGESTION

1 Explore the environment of the drama room in the way the infant explores her environment before walking.

2 Use the senses or as many as you have of touch, taste, smell, sight, hearing, to appreciate the immediate environment of the drama space.

3 Explore the space in as many ways possible, to
   conquer the space, to be overwhelmed by it, to enjoy it
   as an individual and as part of the group.

This kind of exploration through the senses and relaxation
work can be a beginning for many groups; for those who
cannot walk or who have difficulty with movement, the image
and the movement go as far as the movement of the individuals in the group. You adapt the image to the capacity of the
group.

From this beginning the movement of the body can be
explored through the same process as the child learns to move:
rolling, stretched out or curled up, sliding, wriggling, swinging
and falling and rolling.

These are images and movements which I feel comfortable
using and different group leaders must find their own way of
working and their own images which are safe for them and
then they can present them safely for the group.

It is important that the leaders do not impose ideas and
ways of working which they haven't tried out for themselves
because drama is a process, not a series of exercises or games
which you make a group enact. To present drama as a series
of exercises is like making animals jump through hoops with
no respect for the way a group process ideas and stimuli.

Creative themes from sensory awareness

Many creative themes can develop from awareness about the
body and the process of exploring the world through the physical self. Progression to other dramatic material will be at the
pace and skill level of the group. From simple relaxation and
movement play, the group focus will develop through the
themes and images members bring to the group. These themes
will be worked through according to the kind of group that
was initially set up. If the group are meeting as a Creative-
Expressive group then creative material and movement themes
will probably develop. If the group are task based, then perhaps
feelings about the body and how we communicate them to
others may emerge, or maybe play about body boundaries and
touch can be developed in groups who have experienced abuse
of the body in some way.

For example, play with children who have had invasive treat-
ments for life-threatening illnesses could be an exploration of
images about that treatment and the messages given by adults

to be strong and brave. This exploration would have developed from early embodiment play in the group. This could be expressed through group sculpts about treatment processes or more symbolic sculpts of physical power relationships.

Members of another group may want to express their feelings about what their bodies are like and how this affects the way they are treated in social situations, and to develop ways of playing with these themes.

Body work and movement stir so many dramatic images for all of us, especially if others have had control of our bodies or personal bodily functions. If in drama we can explore the world through the senses in safety and begin to know who we are through our bodies then this is the way we begin to explore and find an identity for ourselves.

SUGGESTION

Find a comfortable, closed-up position on the floor.

Close your eyes and keep them closed.

Imagine that you are in a soft, silken cocoon
surrounded by a soft, strong shell that protects you.

Explore your existence inside the cocoon.

Discover how much space you have.

Discover how much you can move around.

Now slowly break out of your cocoon.

Be aware of how you feel when you emerge.

When you emerge begin to stretch your body.

Let your stretching flow into a sound.

Open your eyes and look around at other people.

You have explored being alone in your cocoon, warm
and safe in your shell.

And now open your eyes and view the world outside
and other people in that world.

This exercise is a way to begin to encourage members of the group to relate to each other.

So what do you have to do to make friends?

How do you talk to people?

These are the constant questions from people with special needs. It can be fun to try this out in play.

Just open your eyes, look at someone instead of hiding your eyes.

Just smile at someone in the room.

It's a beginning.

From these early explorations of the kind of person we are physically, what our senses tell us of the world outside, we can begin to explore play through the use of symbols and metaphors which help us make sense of that world 'out there'. We can begin to tell our stories, and try to make sense of ourselves as social beings in the world. This is the beginning of symbolic play.

SYMBOLIC PLAY AND IMPROVISATION

In early childhood, symbolic play is the place where the child first recognises the separateness of what is 'me' and 'not me'. It is the beginning of an exploration of objects and relationships of the world beyond the self. This is the time when children play with toys and objects and use these objects to represent their experience. The way children play symbolically is through dramatic play, making stories and improvising situations to express their world.

All humans use symbols to express things outside the present situation, be they verbal metaphor, body imagery, visual symbols, sounds. Children begin to improvise play about 'things not present' with objects and toys, taking anything to hand, transforming it to use as part of their play.

This symbolic use of objects is of special importance with groups who have limited mobility but can manipulate objects.

Taking an object and imagining it represents something else is the way children develop symbolic understanding which is the way they begin to understand language. In drama the beginning of 'Let's pretend'.

SUGGESTION

Everybody sits in a circle.

One person begins by taking a pencil and, using it in a particular way, shows that the pencil has become something else.

The player mimes the 'something else', a comb, for example.

The rest of the group must guess what the pencil has become.

Then it is passed to the next person who must use it in a different way.

The pencil should be passed round the circle several times.

This play gets the group in touch with the symbolic possibilities of objects.

SUGGESTION

The leader collects small family dolls, sets of plastic animals, dolls' house furniture, etc.

These objects are placed in piles.

Each person is asked to choose a figure or animal, then to draw on a large sheet of paper the place and surroundings where the person/animal lives.

When the drawing is finished, the object can be placed in its environment.

Then, from the other piles of objects, other creatures and objects are selected to people the world.

Now a three-dimensional world has been created.

Each person then describes the world thus created to the rest of the group or in small groups.

The next step can be to make up stories or act a scene about the world of each creature.

Making worlds with objects is an enjoyable way of making dramatic play for both adults and children and can be a safe way to begin symbolic play.

IMPROVISED PLAY

Improvised play can be the next step in the process of experiencing symbolic play in drama. From awareness of our own bodies and sensory exploration of objects which can be used symbolically, we can begin to experiment with stories and improvised scenes integrating those experiences. Viola Spolin (1986) states that the heart of improvisation is transformation. This is the great power of drama, this capacity to transform objects and transform experiences. Improvisation work requires spontaneity, it is a process of doing, where the focus is on action; 'Show, don't tell', is the message. It is important for the leader not to get bogged down in talk about 'doing' in drama groups. This can be a distraction by group members, a process of avoidance of issues or it can be a way of warming-up to the action. The skill of the leader is to know what it is and to encourage the group to play. Once the action has started then the anxiety is focused and it is the job of the leader to help the group to actions which are safe enough for every member of the group but not so safe as to be stultifying. The skill lies in the boundaries and agreements made with the group which will be discussed in Chapter 3.

SUGGESTION

Improvised play often flows from the stimulus of play with objects as in childhood. I found an old handbag in a jumble sale; inside the bag was a purse with a railway ticket to Great Yarmouth dated June 1937 and two old pennies. Each person will find different objects and should

> show the objects,
>
> imagine the life of the owner of the objects,
>
> improvise a story about how the owner might have used the objects,
>
> share the story with the rest of the group.

Over the years you can collect interesting items to stir the imagination. The objects should be powerful enough and connected enough to stir the imagination.

Use visual stimulation, pictures, postcards of paintings, anything which stirs your imagination and this interest will be passed on to some of the group.

SUGGESTION

It is often fun to begin improvisation by setting a scene, perhaps in a park, and delineate the scene in the drama room with ideas from the group.

> Imagine this room is a park.
>
> Let's set the scene.
>
> There is a park bench, pond, paths, flowerbeds, ducks swimming, an ice cream cart and a notice board with the park regulations.

Anyone in the group can come into the park as who you like or an animal if you want, a dog or a duck or a bird.

You meet other people in the park, or perhaps you don't meet, you feed the ducks, or walk, sit on the bench, or what you choose.

You sniff around the park if you are a dog.

But only four people can be in this park at the same time.

As a fifth person arrives one of you must leave.

See how many people or animals move in and out of the park.

This can be a safe way to start improvisation as there is no need to speak or even meet anybody else but everyone can take a role – child, dog, duck, park keeper or whoever.

SUGGESTION
Another simple way of beginning to play in this way is to work in pairs.

One player calls out the name of a place such as, ambulance station or a phone box.

The other player becomes an object associated with the place.

Then the pair enact a short scene, one partner playing an object, the other a person.

These improvisations have their basis in symbolic play and begin to develop an understanding of taking a role as part of the development of the play.

DRAMA GAMES

As children develop dramatic play and their social skills emerge, then games with rules become part of play. The use of drama games for the group develops social roles and inter-play and helps with the understanding that rules can often ease the passage of social relationships because they boundary the communication. It can become a symbolic way to learn the importance of boundaries and what is acceptable behaviour with other people. For those with learning difficulties, for example, this kind of play can help group members with social roles and appropriate body boundaries.

Through playing games group members begin to notice how they are in the group and how the group relate to them. Games require co-operation from everyone in the group and this makes individuals more aware of their own contribution. Games can incorporate all group members, small groups or partners.

SUGGESTIONS
Connecting the group together through forming patterns or moving from small groups into big groups can be a way of creating a cohesive group.

Big Snake

In twos, people lie stretched on their stomachs on the floor.

One holds the ankles of the person in front to make a two-people snake.

This snake slithers across the floor to make a four-people snake.

Then an eight-people snake and so on until the group is one Big Snake.

This snake can then perhaps try to roll over, or stretch in the sun to sleep, or slither into a hiding place or whatever the group enjoys doing the most.

Double bubble

This is a small group play.

Two or three people form a bubble by holding hands together or by any other means which suggest a bubble.

The bubbles then float around the room, careful not to bump into other bubbles in case they pop.

Talking without words

In pairs.

One partner makes nonsense sounds.

The other partner responds with a movement showing how the sounds made her feel.

This produces a conversation.

The two take turns to speak and to respond.

People to people

People choose partners and stand face to face.

The leader calls out 'elbow to knee' or 'nose to finger' and the pairs respond together to the instruction.

When the leader shouts 'people to people' pairs re-form and repeat the game.

A variation called *Face to Face* is played in the same way except that the instructions are for the same body part such as, face to face, toe to toe, back to back, knee to knee, and so on.

It is important to give clear instructions about the rules of games and careful thought must go into choosing games which are playable for people with special needs.

For example, *Face to Face* can be played in wheelchairs if the leader chooses appropriate body parts to meet. Some groups who find big group games complicated may well be able to enjoy games with partners. However, some groups will not have the capacity to make the social interactions necessary to enjoy games in drama.

STORIES

Storymaking is an exciting medium for drama work with individuals and groups. There is such a sense of achievement when someone makes a story which can be shared with another person or a group.

Where children play alone, toys and other objects are often used as the basis for a story. Children quite spontaneously select objects and begin to play in story form. I usually say, 'That sounds like a story to me. How shall I begin? Is it once upon a time?' I offer to write the story for the children as they individually tell or enact one. If the children are not sure how to begin I usually start them off with, 'Once upon a time there was a . . .' and that is enough to set a child off. The stories can be very simple like this one from a boy of 12 with learning difficulties. He was playing with some dolls of the Simpson family, a TV programme, and he wrote:

> Once upon a time there was a family called Simpson and they lived in a house and they are a happy family and don't smell. Dad works in a factory.
>
> Bart was on his skateboard and he knocked down a dustbin. 'Oh no, not again,' he thought 'Oi, look out! You've knocked my dustbin down'.
>
> The man pushed him into the dustbin.
>
> His sister came on the skateboard. He was in the dustbin and his sister came.

This simple story has many meanings for Peter and he was proud of his ability to tell me the story, for me to write it down so he could hear it back. We then acted it with Peter playing the hapless Bart and I played the sister who in the end helped him out of the dustbin.

Mary is 18. She has a severe language disorder and has been severely abused. She told the following short story while playing with dolls and drawing:

> Once upon a time there was a house and in that house lived a girl and a cat. The girl was happy, the cat was sad. One day the cat ran away because he was sad. As he ran down the road he met a man who was horrid and the man hit the cat so it ran home.

This story very much expresses Mary's difficulties about finding a life for herself.

This is John's story. He was abused in his family.

> This is John's house. It is red with just me and Raphael (Ninja Turtle). We make our own food and drinks. We don't speak to anyone. It's not safe in the house. There's too much ghosts. Green slimy ghosts like Slimer and he eats me up and Raphael. The house was empty but we dropped out of Slimer's tummy and ate him up and he is in our tummy now but the house is still not safe.

Stories are a powerful way of helping children make connections with their own experiences. Anger and violent feelings, sadness and pain can be expressed in stories and if an adult can hear the story and accept what is expressed it helps the child understand that powerful feelings can be dealt with by adults without being overwhelmed and engulfed by them.

Children also like to hear stories and act parts of stories from a very early age. 'Three Billy Goats Gruff' was a favourite story for one 4 year old boy who enjoyed being both the troll and the largest Billy Goat. He enjoyed the verbal repetition of:

'Who has been crossing my bridge?' and for once in a story he was powerful always and horrible sometimes yet still those parts of himself expressed in the story were accepted by the adult who watched.

Children will find different things to connect with in a story. I once used Red Riding Hood with a small group of children who were experiencing difficulties with family relationships. One of the most potent parts of the story for that group was the fact that Little Red Riding Hood didn't listen to her mother and stopped to pick flowers in the woods instead of going straight to her granny's house. This part of the story was acted many times with much role reversing. They liked to act the role of the mother, always feeling angry, telling everybody what to do and never being heeded. This was most potent for one child in the group who didn't listen to her mother and didn't go straight home from school. She wandered where the will took her and had got into several scrapes. Her mother constantly shouted at her about this and Janice was able to play familiar scenes through the story of Red Riding Hood. In her fictional world, she could experience the story from the point of view of the mother as well as Red Riding Hood.

SUGGESTIONS

Use stories in meaningful ways for the interests of the group. Help members of the group to expand and explore the story in their own way so it has personal meanings for the group and individuals. For example, I use the story of Terry Jones (1981) called 'Katy-Make-Sure'. I read the story to the group. The gist of the story is as follows:

> There was a little girl called Katy who found an old shoe which belonged to a goblin. He was delighted when the shoe was found because without it he couldn't go back to Goblin City. He offered to take Katy to Goblin City where she would be rewarded by the King of the Goblins.

However Katy wanted to know how they would get there and Goblin's reply was,

Short or long to Goblin City?
The straight way's short
But the long way's pretty!

Katy couldn't make up her mind, should she go the short way or should she go the long way?

The Goblin got angry with her because she couldn't make up her mind.

He says

Goblin City's far and near!
If you want to make sure,
You'd better stay here!

In the end the Goblin leaves her behind so she never got to Goblin City either way.

It is better to read the story from the book *Fairy Tales*.

SUGGESTIONS FOR WORKING WITH THE STORY

Tell the story up to the offer of a reward from the King of the Goblins.

Ask in the group to write what reward they each would like on a piece of paper.

Continue the story up to the end of the Goblin's first rhyme about Goblin City.

Ask all members of the group to draw what they imagine the short way to Goblin City looks like.

Then ask them to draw what they think the long way looks like.

Ask them to make groups of three people.

Suggest that they talk about their drawings with each other.

Continue telling the story until Katy really can't decide which way to go at all. Stop.

Ask the group as Katy to write a letter to her mum explaining the difficulty and asking her advice.

Tell the story to the end.

Organise pairs and ask them to imagine that it is five years later.

'Phone your mum about that letter you wrote those years ago.

Tell her if you took her advice.

Did you somehow or other find your way to Goblin City in the end?

If you went, which way did you go and what reward did you get?

Was it what you wanted?

If you didn't go, do you regret it or not?

Tell your mum on the 'phone.

Take it in turns to be mother and Katy on the 'phone.

Get the whole group together in a circle.

Each person takes on the role of Katy for one minute at the most and tells the group if she made the journey or not.

There are many other ways of using this delightful story. It can be a metaphor for many journeys we made or didn't make and the ways we choose to go or not to go.

For those who can't write then telling it to someone else in the group or drawing is as effective. Use the story in ways which are appropriate for the skill level of the group. To tell the story is enough for some, repeating the rhymes for others. It can be as simple or as complex as the group choose.

Stories to explore cultural identity

Stories are a powerful way for groups to explore their cultural past and formulate pride in their ethnicity. Dramatic skills of a particular culture can be explored and developed and this in turn reinforces the group and individual's sense of confidence in achieving a particular skill and the sense of the specialness of that skill or the specialness of the story.

SUGGESTION

I worked with a group of African boys displaced from a variety of countries. They had witnessed war and violence and the stories which they developed were from Tortoise the Trickster (1979) – see Chapter 4. Some of these stories were about basic survival in a harsh world and the value which appealed to these displaced boys was that you must always look after your mother. Their longing for family and the loss they felt in a different culture were expressed through telling these stories and acting scenes.

The safety of the structure of the stories was also important. These were stories about animals, not people, so they were distanced from their own experiences which they could safely explore through the experiences of the animals.

Narrative therapy: changing the story

Narrative therapy has an interesting structure which could be used as a basis for story work or drama enactment.

This therapy is based on the notion that people continuously give meanings to their lives by making stories about themselves and their relationships.

The concepts of narrative therapy are based on post-modern ideas, in particular that people have no direct access to an objective external reality and what we know is always what we have created through our own ideas and our own construction of the world.

We define our lives by the stories we tell about ourselves. As we relate to significant others in our lives then these relationships form a relational self and this self is continuously defined in our collection of evolving stories.

Some stories are more useful than others but no story is objectively more true than another.

This multiplicity of perspectives is negotiated by the individual and makes it possible to develop and expand the roles a person can play in the story of their life.

In cybernetic theory, G. Bateson (1972) stated that events take their course because they are restrained from taking alternative courses and that people can redefine their relationships against restraints (cultural assumptions, practices and beliefs) by expanding their roles and the drama they play in.

M. White and D. Epston (1989) developed a framework for narrative therapy based on Bateson's cybernetic theories of restraints and information.

This therapy explores the construction and reconstruction of people's lives through a restorying process.

When people define themselves in their stories it can be that some dominant stories are problem saturated and some of these stories are consolidated by significant people in a person's life.

These stories contain restraints which prevent people from noticing new information which might leave them space to perform another story.

This other story is about unique outcomes where the person is able to have some impact over the problem.

If access to unique outcomes is closed then all events are shaped through the dominant story which gives meaning to all experiences.

D. Epston and M. White (1992) developed a variety of techniques to help people make alternative stories of their lives.

Firstly the problem in the dominant story is externalised by separating the person from the problem. The problem is located outside the person or relationship. It is objectified and given a name.

For example, working with a sexually abused boy of 11 who used secrecy to control his relationships, we externalised initially the theme of our drama as 'secrecy' and he constructed his story of friendships controlled by secrecy.

The old story is deconstructed, i.e. questioned, taken apart and then reconstructed to create fuller descriptions and alternative stories for a fuller narrative.

The boy was able to use symbolic stories and dramatic play to examine other ways of making relationships that could give him a wider repertoire of roles to play.

NARRATIVE THERAPY IN A DRAMA GROUP
These ideas could be used in a drama group to examine stories and characters and rework them to define new stories.

The basic process of role talking and storymaking in drama develop an understanding of narrative and the possibility of alternative choices.

The group could take a fairy story such as *Hansel and Gretel* and explore aspects of the story through the three processes of objectifying the problem, deconstructing and reconstructing the story.

The group could focus on a particular aspect of the story, perhaps defining the restraint of poverty, and then explore family alternatives to abandoning the children in the forest to fend for themselves.

Characters in stories could be asked questions about their dominant story which could then be reworked in many ways by the group. What are the restraints for Cinderella with her family of stepsisters and stepmother, or for the Twelve Dancing Princesses and their secret lives, or for Rumpelstiltskin and his desire to control and have power over the miller's beautiful daughter. The group could invent new endings for their stories.

ROLE PLAY

In the developmental exploration of drama process we experience ourselves in drama through the senses, play with objects, symbols outside ourselves. Through improvisations and story-telling we explore situations and roles in more complex ways.

Young children experiment with roles from a very early age. Children are curious to know what it means to be the postman, the fireman, a mother, father, naughty child or Mighty Mouse. In drama we can also explore roles to develop a repertoire of social roles. Drama can be the place to explore some of the inappropriate roles which may have developed through family interactions or difficulties with other social situations.

Through these explorations we can begin to understand the relationship between our internal and external worlds. Role is made up of two parts: your 'self' and the 'other person' that you become. The 'other person' half of the role gives you the safety of exploring ideas and situations quite different from those of your own life. The 'self' half of the role allows you to use your values and responses in the drama situation to understand what has happened. When you balance the 'other' person part of the role that you are given to play in drama with the 'self' part of the role you can believe in the role that you are playing.

The techniques of drama centre on transformation: how people can turn into other people or other beings in order to create a there-and-then story in a here-and-now place. We are making fiction in drama but when we make fiction there has to be a life in it. That is the paradox of drama. In life we play a little, in fiction we live a little.

SUGGESTION

Family role play

Exploration of family misunderstandings.

A scene with 16 year old son or daughter and father or mother.

Set the scene.

Mother and daughter have been arguing a lot recently.

Daughter has been staying out late and been rude to mother who has also been irritable and tense.

Mother is anxious about her daughter and comes to her bedroom to talk.

She opens her daughter's bedroom door. She doesn't knock first.

Daughter has been feeling unsettled, waiting for her exam results, not knowing what she wants to do.

She has enjoyed the summer with friends and is not looking forward to going back to school.

Yet she knows she has been difficult and bad tempered all through the summer.

She is sitting in her bedroom, mother bursts into her room without knocking.

Having set the scene give the following information to the mother.

You go into your daughter's bedroom and see her quickly hide a tin box under her bed. You are worried about her friends. Do they take drugs?

Instructions to daughter

You feel bad about your behaviour during the summer and have bought your mother a present of an antique box which you know she would like. You are about to wrap it up to give to her when she barges into your room without knocking.

This role play can show how easily misunderstandings occur. After playing the scene discuss what happened. Talk about the roles people played, keep in the fiction of the drama. It is important not to mix up role playing with 'real' life. In social role play as in any other taking of a dramatic role, we are making a fiction and should explore what has happened in the playing as fiction.

Once the scene has been played, the group can experiment with a variety of ways of playing the scene and explore different family dynamics. In drama it is not necessary to find some ideal family or perfect relationship. just to explore fictional lives in all their variety.

Role play with groups with special needs can explore the way the family or society makes assumptions about the role of the 'sick', 'ill' or 'different' person and what it means to the individual to be encapsulated into a role because of society's need to label.

In drama the whole dynamic can be explored – the best part of the role play for the diabetic group was when they could be the parenting figures of consultant/hospital staff and be as bossy to us as they had endlessly experienced in their frequent visits to hospital. They created fictional characters. For once they were playing the adults who were in charge and instead of being told what to do as was their experience in real life, they took the dominant and controlling roles in drama. Being diabetic meant they had so many rules to observe in order to maintain their health; it was a good feeling that in drama they could play those people who were always telling them what to do instead of playing themselves receiving information and advice. What a powerful charge that was!

3

Organisation

BEGINNINGS

GROUP OR INDIVIDUAL WORK

Drama work can take place with a group of people and also with two people. The two people can be equal participants or spectator and player although even in those circumstances the spectator should participate in the drama work at the request of the player. It is important to recognise that in the drama process the spectator who may be the helper is also always the spectator, not the judge but 'one who shares'.

When drama is first considered, it is important to work out why drama is appropriate for the group or individual with special needs. Sometimes individuals need to make sense of some of their life experiences in individual work before they feel they can join a group. Or perhaps the healing process can be met with both individual and group work. For example, young children who have been sexually abused could join a task group where play is about keeping safe from further abuse and learning about body boundaries and individual play could address the specific issues of the child's abuse and the stress that has caused.

Both forms of help could be through dramatic play but with different forms and ways of playing.

DRAMA AS PART OF A
TREATMENT PROGRAMME

For many people the drama group may be part of a wider treatment programme so the work must be integrated into that programme. It can be very helpful for individuals in a drama group to have another place to examine personal issues that arise in the group.

It is important for all those who are involved in running the programme to get together and keep information flowing so that the client is not confused by a mass of conflicting information and help. The treatment programme should be consistent and interventions timed to be helpful, not confusing. There should be an appropriate sharing of information about the needs of the client without breaking confidentiality. If a drama group is decided to be an appropriate way of helping then it must be decided what kind of group to offer.

QUESTIONS TO ANSWER BEFORE STARTING A DRAMA GROUP

Are there enough resources to start a group?

Remember the effectiveness and outcome of a group are in some part determined by the environment in which it might exist.

Do you have support from the organisation of which the group will be part?

What is the degree of co-operation from others in the organisation and other agencies which you might need to form a group?

Are those agencies convinced that a group is needed?

Are there suitable clients for such a group?

Is drama the most appropriate form for this group?

What are the aims of the group?

Can the needs of the group be met through the use of drama?

Is drama the main focus of help?

What group model will be appropriate?

Will it be a closed group from the beginning?

Will new people be able to join? If so, when?

Is it an open group with no specific contract to attend?

What is the focus of the group?

What kind of drama focus will meet the needs of the group?

Will it be a Creative-Expressive group?
A Task Based group?
A Self Advocacy group?

Numbers of participants and leaders/helpers

How many people will be in the group?
What are the minimum and maximum numbers?
Will there be one leader or co-leadership?
Will there be helpers?
What is the ratio of helpers to clients?
If helpers are used what is their role?
Are they participants in drama or there to assist the leader?

Time, duration and frequency of the group

How many sessions will be offered?
In blocks of ten weeks? If so how many blocks, one or two?
Does the group run throughout the year?
Does the group meet once a week, more often, less often?
How long does each group meeting last?
Is it one hour, one and a half hours or two hours?

Selection of group membership

How is the group selected?
Are people referred by professionals or is it self referral or both?
Are people interviewed by the leaders before they join the group?

Publicity

How is the group publicised?
Is the publicity inviting and is the information on the publicity sufficient and accurate?
Who is given the information about the group?

Management of the group

Who is responsible for the management of the group?

Is it the leader, staff team or head of the institution?

Who is responsible for the supervision of the staff?

If the group is part of a Treatment Programme, who co-ordinates the programme?

Setting for the group

Where will the group be held?

Who is responsible for the space, the leader or the manager?

Who else uses the space and what happens to the space just before the group meets?

What happens in accidents and emergencies?

Is there a First Aid Box?

Is there a telephone available?

Who clears up and/or locks up?

These are some of the questions that group facilitators need to ask before beginning. If there is clarity from the facilitators then this enhances the safety of the group and its chance of success.

PLANNING AND PREPARATION FOR THE GROUP

If the drama group are to be helpful then the work must be carefully prepared so that the safety of everybody, group members, leaders and helpers is maintained. This does not mean that the group are forced into rigidity but each session should have an overall structure and the series of meetings should also be linked by ideas and themes relevant to the aims of the group.

The leader who has limited experience of drama will need to prepare very carefully, perhaps over-prepare, so that if the group reject the material offered then the leader has other ideas with which to explore the themes concerning the group.

THE STRUCTURE OF A DRAMA SESSION

It is important that the leader understands the need for a clear structure in a drama session to help the group members through the process of making a piece of drama. This structure for holding the group should be balanced by the ability of the leader to create a mood and environment which can stimulate the work.

This is a delicate balance to achieve. Too much structure, no flexibility means very limited interaction between group members and the leader, too much control from the leader with no capacity to respond to the needs and mood of the group. Too much stimulation without a drama form in which to work can create a heightened level of anxiety which can lead to an immediate discharge of tension and the group runs wild. This is the reactive response to tension as a way to re-establish equilibrium. Response to lack of equilibrium can be fight or flight and the work is put aside. In that situation the group never develop the drama but get lost in the anxiety.

STAGES IN THE DRAMA PROCESS

There are three stages in a drama process for helping and healing.

Warm-up

The first stage is the warm-up period and sets the mood. It is a preparation time for drama, for being in the group and for meeting each other. For the leader it is a way of observing the group dynamics and becoming sensitised to the ideas, themes and feelings which create a focus for the drama. From this warm-up the group proceed to the next stage which is to develop the area of work to be explored by the group.

The phases of the process should flow seamlessly and this can be facilitated by the leader who can help channel ideas to keep the focus clear.

Development phase

This is the phase of creative explorations and enactments. Themes, ideas and feelings are explored through appropriate drama forms. The leader must ensure the safety of the group by selection of appropriate drama material, making sure the ground rules, boundaries and limits are observed together.

This development period is usually absorbing unless the drama form doesn't hold the stimulus. Then the artistic skill of the leader is needed to suggest ways of integration or if that fails other drama forms in which to work.

It is important that the drama form is appropriate for the theme to be explored but, more important, that it is safe for the client. For example, I worked with a 14 year old boy called John who only felt safe doing mime. If I suggested other drama forms, he felt pressurised. He would become disturbed and was unable to settle. But he could channel his feelings through mime. The value was twofold: he learnt to reach for and express his feelings, not explode with them and he was skilled in mime which raised his self esteem and so for him began an exploration of who he was. Through his skill at mime, John was able to find something to like about himself and a way to define himself: 'I'm John and I'm good at mime.'

Closure

The third stage is the final resolution of the drama as the group choose to present it. If the balance between the structure and the stimulus has been achieved, the stimulus held and centred in the drama, then the group will have experienced the process of using drama to express feelings. Finally the group can talk about their work together and evaluate the experience.

DETAILING THE PROCESS

Stage One: the beginning moments

This stage can be the most demanding for the leader who starts out to stimulate emotional arousal in the group yet must boundary the work so the group feel safe enough to hold on and not discharge until the arousal can be placed in the form of the drama. For many group members, holding on to heightened awareness can provoke high anxiety. It is a critical time: too much anxiety and the group members begin to resist, motivation drops and everything stops. We have all experienced moments like this.

EXAMPLE

I remember beginning to work on an entertainment at a conference. The group had prepared material and were coming together for the first time, anxious and insecure. One person began to express doubts about the material and everybody in the group became anxious. All ideas and creative development of the material ceased. The whole group became paralysed with anxiety and cancelled the project. Terror is infectious.

Warm-ups to relieve tension

With some groups who have difficulty holding on to feeling which is unfocused it can be useful to discharge this tension at the beginning of the meeting through an energetic game.

EXAMPLE

I worked with a group of disaffected boys in school and they came to the sessions full of frustrations and suppressed energy from being at school. Sent to the group with this label they came to the room resentful and anxious. We always began with a fast, energetic game, not too competitive to set up more tension but fast enough play to discharge tension and get immediate relief from their generalised frustration. Once they had released that frustration and were physically tired and relaxed they began the drama. The game was carefully selected and the play monitored so that the tension was not projected onto other people rather than released onto the game. Very competitive games can produce more anger.

When a group has been established over several meetings work can be planned for some time ahead with specific objectives according to the initial agreement made with everybody about the reason for establishing the group in the first place. Even with a well-established group it is still important to establish the emotional state of each person at the beginning of a session. The leader must work at the safe level for the most vulnerable members and who they are obviously changes from meeting to meeting. Each person should feel safe enough to contribute as much as possible.

There are always some weeks when the planned work of the leader must be thrown aside because of the group situation; the leader must be flexible and always have enough creative ideas to change plans as the situation dictates.

Once the plan for the drama has been agreed – this can take considerable time to negotiate – the leader should suggest ways of working. Sometimes the leader will start the activity by taking a role in the drama, other times the group will want to work in a corner. The leader should respect and encourage different ways of working, be available when asked, keep the group safe by observing the interactions, but not push in and take over.

Stage Two: giving form to feeling

In the second stage of the process, ideas will be shaped and made particular by the group as members put their own feelings and experiences into the drama. There is much tentative experimentation with form at this stage as the group try out dramatic ideas. Some ideas are discarded, others developed until the participants are satisfied.

EXAMPLE

With one group of adolescent girls I brought a series of pictures. Members of the group worked in pairs, choosing a picture that appealed and each pair made a short scene to show the theme in the picture. Jane and Margaret, two 12 year old girls, chose the picture of a man in a straightjacket as the stimulus to make their scene.

In the improvisation Jane played the person in the straightjacket in prison for so long she didn't know why she was there. She was rescued by Margaret playing the role of a male psychiatrist, who freed the prisoner and took her home. The psychiatrist then hypnotised the girl to discover her past crime which was killing her mother in self defence after a violent quarrel.

The psychiatrist then taught the girl how to cook. One day the psychiatrist fell ill and the girl cooked for him but because the psychiatrist hadn't taught her properly, he died, poisoned. The girl was arrested for murder and ended up in prison in a straightjacket.

From the stimulus of the picture, Jane and Margaret created a drama with strands of their own lives transformed through their story. Jane had recently seen a psychiatrist with her mother and sister after the break-up of her parents' violent marriage. These actual events were symbolically woven with images from the picture. The two girls worked intensely, quite absorbed, sketching out the scene many times, refining the structure until they were both satisfied. They negotiated with each other to include images and ideas that were important to each and particular intense experiences of both girls were expressed and represented in the improvisation they created. Their commitment was balanced because they had negotiated with each other. For both girls, working and presenting their drama was a healing experience. They were expressing feelings about their own lives but in a symbolic form which kept them safely distanced from showing direct experience which would have been far too painful for both of them. They were both absorbed by their story as an artistic endeavour and wanted to develop their story dramatically. They were proud of their enactment.

Stage Three: resolution
The third stage is the final resolution of the drama to the satisfaction of the participants and then the validation of the experience by the group. When this is completed, the material is put into focus by the group and 'owned' by the participants. It is laid to rest. Then the participants start to distance themselves from their creation and separate from the group.

The leader facilitates this process through help with feedback, evaluation and reflexion.

CONTRACT WITH THE GROUP

A contract is a working agreement between the group leader and members of the group. It is a statement of the agreed purpose of the group and that the group is a shared and co-operative venture. All areas of the group's organisation, the nature of the group, its duration, timing, etc., can be negotiated as part of the contract.

The contract could include the following:

1 What is the shared understanding of the aims of the group?
2 The form of drama work to achieve those aims.
3 Knowledge of the skills of the leader and the skills of the group members.
4 Is it a closed or open group?
5 What are the times and duration of the meetings?
6 What are the boundaries and ground rules?
7 How will the rules be maintained?

Boundaries and safety of the group
The safety and security of the group are largely determined by the ground rules that make up the contract between the leader and the group.

Ground rules

The ground rules are the limitations and boundaries agreed by the group at the beginning. They provide a method of learning about the group from the beginning and determine a code of acceptable behaviour.

In a drama group the ground rules could include some of the following:

Respect for everyone's ideas.

Listening to each other and the presentation of ideas not valued as good or bad.

Focus on subject at hand.

Group sharing.

Expression and acceptance of feelings.

Development of trust appropriate to the group.

Genuineness, be yourself.

Acceptance of each other's points of view.

Participation, talking, listening, working through the drama process.

Confidentiality.

Safety of environment, e.g. Who comes into the room?

ARE YOU READY TO BEGIN?

If all the preparations and organisation are achieved, there are people who want to join the group and there is support and recognition from co-workers and institutions, then you are ready to begin.

WORKING WITH INDIVIDUALS

Drama work with individuals requires as much preparation and organisation as working with a group in drama. Ask the same questions as for the group.

Is drama appropriate for this person and how will it meet her needs?

What does the individual think about play and drama?

The way the worker introduces the idea of play and drama is critical especially in individual work with older children and adults.

Is play part of a treatment programme?

How can the programme be integrated and the confidentiality of the individual respected?

Is play as a healing process understood and respected by other workers?

(I remember being told by a judge in court that what I did with children was what nannies used to do.)

What is the focus of the work?

Is it free dramatic play?

Is it task-based work, for example learning about 'good touches' and 'bad touches'?

Is it a combination of free play and task-based play?

Helpers

Is it appropriate to have a helper to care for the special needs of the child?

If so, what is the helper's role? Playing, helping the individual or helping the worker?

What are the rules about confidentiality for the helper?

Selection of clients

Are individuals referred by professionals?

Can individuals refer themselves?

What discussion is there with the client before the sessions begin?

Supervision of the work

Who supervises the work and its emotional impact on the worker?

What training do the worker and supervisor have in drama for helping and healing? (See training courses for dramatherapy and playtherapy in Appendix.)

Setting for the work

Is the space appropriate for play and drama?

Is it a shared space?

How secure is it from interruption?

(See Chapter 10 for description of methods of work with individuals.)

Timing and frequency of the sessions

Most individual sessions are of one hour's duration on a weekly or fortnightly basis.

How many sessions?

It is appropriate to work in blocks of ten sessions then assess.

PLANNING AND PREPARATION FOR PLAY/DRAMA WITH INDIVIDUALS

Planning and preparation for individual work will include selection of themes and materials to reinforce those themes for task-based work and selection of toys and other objects appropriate for non-directive play.

Thought must be given to ways of using the material and making the individual comfortable with play. Most children need no help in this direction.

Structure of a session

The structure of a session flow in the same way as a group drama session. There is a Warm-up, then a Development Phase and finally Closure of the session.

Warm-up

In non-directive play it takes the form of renewing the relationship between client and worker and setting out the room with what is of interest to the client and starting to play.

In a task-based session, the worker may introduce a game or exercise which will focus the client onto the theme of the session.

Development phase

In non-directive work the client may focus on particular objects and develop a story or a dramatic enactment with materials. Sometimes the worker can help the client channel play in order to focus on an appropriate theme.

With task-based work the theme is developed by interactions between client and worker who use appropriate media as in any drama work.

Closure

This is the reflective period and material is selected which focuses the client to the end of play.

In the case of free play, tell the client there is time to play with one more object/toy and try to focus onto reflective material.

Usually we finish with a drawing or embodiment play with Playdoh or such material.

CONTRACT WITH THE INDIVIDUAL

As with a group, this is a working statement of the agreed purpose of playing together, that it is a shared venture and that we co-operate with each other.

We could negotiate some of the following:

1 the form of playing,
2 whether the sessions are open or closed,
3 the time and duration of the sessions,
4 the boundaries.

Ground rules

These will be defined as acceptable behaviour between client and worker and could include:

1 respect for each other,
2 no hitting,
3 no fighting,
4 listening and sharing,
5 saying what you feel,
6 accepting each other's point of view,
7 confidentiality,
8 safety of the room – who comes in.

ARE YOU READY TO START?

Have you have gathered together your materials?

Do you feel the workplace is safe and secure?

Are you clear about the aims and objectives?

Is your client clear about the aims and objectives?

Have you made the ground rules?

Are you supported and your work supervised?

4

Drama to explore cultural identity

Britain has a rich variety of ethnic groups. The largest minority groups are defined by the 1981 Census as 4 per cent 'New Commonwealth', that is Black, with Chinese, Greek Cypriot, Polish, Italian and Irish people as the other major groups.

RACISM IN BRITAIN

Racism can be defined as 'the belief in the inherent superiority of one race over all others and thereby the right to dominance'. (Lorde, 1984, page 115)

We are a racist society and ethnic minorities continue to experience institutional, individual and cultural racism. The people who experience the most virulent expressions of racism are black, of Asian, African and Caribbean origin. While racism is certainly experienced by the other ethnic minorities, it is clear from research that being black in Britain means experiencing racism at its worst.

CULTURAL RACISM

Cultural racism is centred around those values, beliefs and ideas which suggest the superiority of white culture; that other ways of life, in particular the Black British way of life, are somehow 'inferior'. These cultural values permeate society, they reinforce both individual and institutional racism. Many black people internalise these values of a white society in which blackness is denigrated. I meet with many groups and individual children who see a white skin as superior, children who draw and paint themselves as white and see no beauty or value in their own physical presence.

TOWARDS A MULTI-RACIAL SOCIETY

I am not black so cannot speak on behalf of black people. I have no direct experience of oppression as experienced by black people. I cannot presume to put my solutions as a white person onto black communities but equally if I am to confront and deal with my own racism I cannot 'dump' the problem of racism back onto black people and expect them to find the solution, as though they were responsible for the problem in the first place.

So I can listen and share my skills in drama in the ways black people want to use them. I can help people make the journey to discover self esteem and beauty in themselves. And we can all build bridges between cultures to begin to understand each other.

TRAINING FOR FACILITATORS

Before beginning to work on cultural issues with black ethnic groups, or other ethnic groups, it is very important for facilitators in drama who are white people, to undergo training so they can examine and begin to understand the oppression experienced by black ethnic minorities and other minorities. We need to learn and have respect and appreciation for the plurality of culture we are fortunate to have in our society. We need to understand some of the strategies we use to perpetuate racism so that we can monitor our own behaviour as group facilitators.

The following are some strategies listed by Lena Dominelli (1988).

Strategies which perpetuate racism

Denial
This is a refusal to accept that racism exists especially in its institutional and cultural forms, and a statement that racism is a prejudice of very few people.

Omission
Those who refuse to see the racial dimension in social interaction and relate to others as if racism didn't exist.

Decontextualisation
An acceptance that racism exists but not here. Somewhere 'out there' in other countries.

The colour-blind approach
Black people are treated as if they were the same as white people thus negating black people's experience of racism.

Dumping
The responsibility of racism is placed on black people who are blamed for what is happening.

The patronising approach
White ways are thought superior, black ways are tolerated but clearly thought inferior.

Avoidance
An awareness of race as a factor of social interaction but confronting it is avoided. When racist behaviour is observed people keep quiet about it.

It is important that these strategies should be explored and awareness of racism and its oppression should be acknowledged: that it is not 'out there' but within our society and ourselves.

DRAMA GROUPS TO DEVELOP SELF ESTEEM AND EXPLORE CULTURAL IDENTITY

Drama can be a powerful way for individuals and groups to develop self esteem and identity. If I am asked to work with such a group or individuals I find out what role models they have from their own ethnic group. If a group have few black role models in the community then I would try to find a black person or individual from the ethnic community of the group to act as facilitator and role model. If the community or the family of people in the group were from the same ethnic background, then they would have good role models in the ethnic group and I would feel able to act as facilitator.

SELF ESTEEM WORK WITH CHILDREN

For any work on the self esteem of the group to be successful the group must feel comfortable and safe, know the rules and limits and what is expected. This atmosphere is created by the way the facilitator builds relationships and creates a caring environment and by the ground rules set at the beginning of the life of the group.

When the environment has been established, people can explore their sense of their own individuality through their understanding of their physical self, their skills and qualities and the roles they take. From this beginning the individual develops a feeling of belonging to the group and begins to discover shared interests and skills.

When the ground rules include listening to each other and respect for each other's point of view, children begin to feel competent and valued for their strengths and can acknowledge their weaknesses as individuals and as members of the group.

Successful working together involves establishing a shared experience from the beginning so warm-up games are very important to create a feeling of group solidarity.

EXAMPLE

Catch the Dragon's Tail

Players line up with arms round the waist of the person in front.

Last one has a scarf in her pocket.

The player at the front of the line tries to grab the scarf.

No part of the Dragon may break.

This kind of game, of which there are many, creates a physical solidarity but not too much conflict. Playing can release tension and anxiety and warm up the group for action.

Name games

Working with young children to develop self esteem we must begin with names. The first response to 'Who am I?' is your name. It is important that other people respect your name, can pronounce it properly and can spell it.

I worked with one young boy who constantly forgot his last name and said he couldn't write or spell it, so the play we did together at the beginning of our time together was to help him take pride in his name and be able to write and spell it. When he accepted his name he began to respect himself.

This is who I am

> The group stand in a circle.
>
> They take turns to stand in the middle.
>
> The person in the middle gives a name, a sound and a movement.
>
> Everyone imitates the person in the middle while she watches.
>
> Another person stands in the middle.

For young children, just say the name and make a simple movement, or say the name and make a sound. Three things to do and imitate can be too complicated for some.

This game helps people own themselves and the gestures and sounds indicate their feelings about themselves and their place in the group.

Singing songs and changing names

> The group sit down together and sing songs, using their own names instead of the name in the song.
>
> The children are asked to suggest the song or rhymes: 'Mary, Mary, quite contrary', 'Jack and Jill went up the hill', 'Polly, put the kettle on.'
>
> Then they use their own names instead.

Play develops from names to the theme of My Body.

My body

FACE

> Work in small groups.
>
> Encourage each child to look in the mirror.
>
> Talk with the group about what their faces look like.
>
> Describe the skin colour and texture.
>
> Describe the facial features from forehead down to the neck.
>
> Describe hair colour, texture, length.
>
> Talk about the way different people look after their skin and hair.

This orientates the children to look carefully at themselves and to note similarities and differences with others in the group.

Watch my face

Everybody in a circle.

One player makes a crazy face and sends it round the circle one way.

When the first face is going round she starts another face and sends it round the other way.

When each face has gone round the circle another person begins.

This can be tried with sounds as well.

My face

Make sure you have a variety of paints, crayons, etc. with which to paint a variety of skin colours.

Draw a picture of your face after looking at it in the mirror.

Decorate your drawing using paint and scrap material like hair, string and wool.

Show the pictures and talk about the different skin colours in the group.

Feeling faces

Make sure you have a wide variety of paints which can define skin colours of group members.

Draw two pictures of your face.

Show a happy face.

Show an angry face

Put your happy face picture in front of your face and make a statue with your body to show how you look feeling happy.

Do the same with your angry face.

Add a happy sound and an angry sound.

Share your statues with the group.

HANDS

In pairs.

Children sit facing each other, with crossed legs.

One claps a rhythm.

The partner joins in and together they keep up the rhythm hitting the floor and their knees.

Then they try it again with music.

LEGS AND FEET

The feet dance

The group are wearing track suits or jeans.

They lie flat on their backs with legs in the air.

With slow rhythmic movement, they let their legs dance in the air, first slowly, then fast, then slowly again.

Walking on different surfaces

Imagine you are walking with bare feet over: warm sand, cold pebbles, cold slime, hot sharp stones.

Group walk changing rhythm

The group walk round the room not bumping into each other.

The leader beats a drum and the group keep the rhythm.

The leader changes the rhythm and the group change their walk accordingly.

HAIR

Mum in a hurry

Choose a partner.

Make a scene with Mum trying to tidy your hair just before school.

The hairdresser's shop

The group set up a hairdresser's shop.

Customers enter and want to have their hair done.

One hairdresser is bossy and hurts a customer by pulling her hair.

What happens?

WHOLE BODY

The skeleton

The leader describes the body and the skeleton.

The leader reads aloud the book *Funnybones* by Janet and Allan Ahlberg (1980/90).

The group talk about the story and the way the skeleton fits together.

They get into small groups of three who imagine they are the Funnybones family.

They talk about what they are going to do tonight.

They make up a story about the Funnybones family and show it to the larger group.

The body

Pinocchio

Partners.

One partner is a puppet on the ground unable to move.

The other child is the puppeteer and moves the puppet by pulling imaginary strings.

Feeling sculpture

Partners.

One partner whispers a feeling word like angry, sad, silly to the other who makes a sculpture of the feeling.

They then see whether another pair of partners can guess what the feeling is.

The whole self

Self portrait

Find a partner.

Ask the following questions and write or tell the answers.

The questions are about 'What do I look like?'

What colour are your eyes?

Do you have freckles?

Do you wear glasses?

Are you left-handed or right-handed?

Is your hair long/short/curly/straight?

What is your favourite colour for clothes?

How do I measure up?

Partners

Take a measuring tape and measure parts of your body.

Put the answers on paper or tell your partner. Write your name.

From head to foot I measure . . .

Round my neck I measure . . .

Round my waist I measure . . .

Round my wrist I measure . . .

How different are you from your partner?

What do you wish for yourself?

If you had three wishes what would they be?

If you could change how you look what would you change?

What is the best thing that could happen to you?

What would you change about people who look after you?

What would you change about where you live?

If you weren't yourself who would you like to be?

Interviews

Partners

One person interviews the other. Ask the following questions or make up some for yourself.

Show it to the rest of the group.

Perhaps you could tape it or video it.

How old are you?

Where do you live?

What do you do at home in your spare time?

What is your favourite food?

What is your favourite place to go for an outing?

There are many such games and activities to help the children in a group to develop pride in themselves and have an understanding of themselves as people whose ideas, views and feelings are valued and recognised.

SHARING CULTURAL CELEBRATIONS

This is one of the ways to develop an understanding and respect for the plurality of cultures in multi-ethnic Britain but it must be done in a wholehearted way with genuine interest not just be tokenism.

For example, one of the difficulties experienced by parents of children in nurseries where I worked in London was the unequal emphasis placed on Christmas and the pressure this brought to families of religions other than Christian. For children of these families Christmas, compared to their own religious festivals, appeared so much more rewarding, with lots of excitement, parties and present giving.

There seemed to be the double message of acknowledging the festivals of other faiths and ethnic communities but still reinforcing the superiority of Christmas with more money being allocated for that celebration.

However, one of the most successful sharing of cultures was undertaken in those nurseries when with the help of parents each child's birthday was celebrated in the way of that ethnic group and the parents gave recipes, contributed the appropriate food and talked to the children about the ceremonies around birthdays. Songs were sung, and ceremonies enacted. Many parents made tapes of stories and translations of texts were written in appropriate languages in picture books.

SHARING STORIES

Stories are an exciting way of reinforcing self esteem in children, developing pride in a living culture by reviving the oral tradition. Happily there are now many artists/performers from ethnic groups who train and perform and use their cultural references to link past stories to present living. Exciting use of theatre and dramatic forms, music and dance enliven and broaden the whole cultural spectrum.

The stories that follow are ones which have interested groups and individuals and connected past and present in powerful ways. Sometimes we have just brought and told stories together, other times acted the story or used it as a stimulus by the group to create another story or ritual which had meaning for the group.

Stories can be just for telling, helping the group get in touch with their cultural past. There are themes which can be explored in drama, drawing and play, and there is history to be learnt. I have taken examples of African, Afro-American and Arab stories which have been enjoyed.

The themes in African tales are the contrast between the order of the village and the wildness of the bush and the protection of the family valued above all. The stories were performed with interruptions and vocal responses from the audience. The players used dancing, singing, drumming and acting (with costumes and masks). This can be an exciting way to explore the stories.

Afro-American stories are from communities of Afro-Americans established in America during the plantation times. These stories emerged throughout a huge area where plantations were worked: South and Central America, the Caribbean and the southern United States. These tales show the endurance of enslaved people who remembered their cultural traditions and maintained and developed them in the face of slavery and oppression. There is fun in the stories and the enjoyment of trickery to get your own back on the powerful Masa King.

Arab stories were told at night, when darkness fell and the women were stitching, that was the time for women and children to hear the stories. For men, stories were often told by the professional storytellers in markets and coffee houses.

There was, there was not,
Shall we tell stories
Or sleep in our cots?

African Stories

Oh No, Not My Mother (Cameroon)

There was once a terrible famine in the country. Nobody had enough to eat, people and animals were dying so the animals called a meeting. They discussed the famine and what to do. Then Hare said, 'There is only one solution. We must eat our mothers. They have lived long and will be glad to give us life a second time.' All the animals agreed. Now Tortoise was at the meeting. He loved his mother very much. He wondered what he might do. That night when the animals were asleep he took his mother and hid her in the clouds because he could not bear to eat her. He gave her a long rope and a basket and said he would come every afternoon to give her food.

The animals met each day and ate the meat from the body of the chosen animal mother. Each day Tortoise saved some meat for his mother and took it to her calling, 'Send down the basket, Mammy', and she did and was fed. Gradually the animals used up their supply of meat. Tortoise knew that one day the animals would ask about his mother, so one morning he ran to the meeting crying saying, 'My mother is dead. She has died of hunger. Come and see the small grave where I buried her.'

The animals comforted Tortoise and after a visit to the grave went to their meeting. But Hare began to watch Tortoise and saw him keep some meat aside so Hare followed Tortoise and watched him call to his Mammy and put food in the lowered basket.

Hare rushed back to the other animals and told them what he had seen. The animals decided that the next day they would wait until Tortoise had given his mother food and when he was asleep Leopard would call for the basket to be lowered, climb into it, go up to the cloud, capture mother Tortoise and eat her. The next day they did as planned but Mammy Tortoise was as clever as her son and when she heard the loud voice of Leopard she knew it wasn't her son and did not lower her basket.

The animals realised that Leopard's voice was too loud so they sent him to the blacksmith to get his voice made smaller. He had to go twice until his voice was small enough but when for the third time he stood under Mammy Tortoise's basket she thought it was her son and lowered the basket. Leopard jumped in with all the other animals and told Mammy Tortoise to raise the basket.

She began to pull the basket up. It was very heavy; she thought her son must have got a lot of food for her. While she was still pulling up the basket Tortoise woke. He looked around but could see no one so he rushed to his mother's cloud because he suspected something might be wrong. When he got there he saw the basket half way up to his mother and guessed what had happened. He shouted to his mammy, 'It wasn't me who called you, Mammy. Cut the rope, cut the rope.'

Mammy Tortoise got a knife and cut the rope and, 'Wap', the basket fell to the ground killing all the animals. Tortoise and his mammy had plenty of meat and never went hungry again.

Themes

The value placed on family.

Survival in extreme conditions.

This story was powerful for African boys who had come from Uganda and had experienced unspeakable horrors. It spoke for them in a strong way and helped them share some of their terrors.

Leopard, Goat and Ram

A man was running away from his village and he took all his property with him. This was a leopard, a goat and a ram. He came to a river where there was only one canoe. This canoe was so small he could only take one animal at a time. How could he get all his property to the other side? If he left the yam with the goat or the leopard with the goat, the goat would eat the yam or the leopard eat the goat.

This is what he did. He took the goat over first and then the yam. He then recrossed the goat, and took over the leopard returning finally for the goat.

WORKING WITH THE STORY

Warm-up

Partners

Cross the room in as many ways as you can think of as a pair but only ever put two feet on the ground, e.g. piggyback, one stands on the feet of the other who walks across.

Development

Leader tells the story. Group act the story.

Act the story with 'What would happen if?' e.g. the goat kicked a hole in the canoe.

Develop other stories about getting people/objects across rivers.

Take the theme from Africa to where the group are now. Perhaps pretend that they are moving house – getting the wardrobe up the stairs. Then they pretend they are crossing the road instead of crossing the river. It is a busy road and they have a dog, the baby and six parcels.

Wondrous Powers. Mirror, Sandals and a Medicine Bag

An old man had three children, all boys. He called the boys and told them he was too old to provide for them or for himself. He ordered them to go out and bring food and clothing.

The three set out and when they came to a large river they went their separate ways The eldest told the youngest to take the middle road, the second to go to the right and he himself would take the left road. Then in a year's time they would meet at the same spot.

At the end of the year they met again. The eldest asked the youngest what he had got on his travels. The youngest said, 'I have nothing but a mirror but it has wonderful powers. If you look in it you can see all over the country no matter how far away.'

The second brother said that all he had was a pair of sandals but if you put them on you could walk to any part of the country in one step.

Then the eldest said that all he had obtained was a small calabash of medicine. But let us look in the mirror and see how our father is.

They all looked into the mirror and saw that their father was already dead and the funeral ceremonies completed. Then the elder said let us hurry home to see what we can do. So the second brought out the sandals and all three put their feet inside, and immediately they were at their father's grave. Then the eldest took out his medicine and shook it over the grave. At once their father rose up as if nothing had ever been the matter with him.

Now which of these three sons has performed the best?

USING THE STORY

Develop any of the following:

Make up stories or draw about how each brother got his special piece of magic.

In groups of three take the role of one of the brothers and explain to the others why you performed the best.

Talk about the value of sharing skills.

In threes. Make up a story and show the others about crossing a river with each person offering a special skill to help the three get across.

Afro-American stories

Getting Common Sense (Jamaica)

Once upon a time Anansi thought that he could collect all the common sense in the world and keep it for himself and in that way he would get plenty of money and plenty of power because everyone would have to come to him with their problems and he would charge them for his advice. Anansi started to collect up and up all the common sense he could find and put it together into one big calabash. He decided to put the calabash on top of a tall tree so nobody could find it.

So Anansi tied a rope to the end of the calabash, tied the two ends of the rope together and hung the rope round his neck so that the calabash balanced on his belly.

He started to climb the tall tree but couldn't climb very well or very fast because the calabash got in the way. He was trying very hard when all of a sudden he heard a voice burst out laughing at the back of him. And when he looked he saw a little boy standing under the tree. 'What a foolish man! If you want to climb the tree front ways why don't you put the calabash behind you?'

Well, Anansi was so angry to hear such common sense from such a little boy when he thought he had collected all the common sense in the world that Anansi took the calabash, broke it into pieces and the common sense scattered out all over the world;

Everybody got a little piece of it but nobody got it all. It was Anansi that made it so.

Themes

What is common sense?

Which bit of common sense did you get?

Which bit of common sense would you like that you haven't got?

Find a partner. Imagine one of you is a shopkeeper who has a shop full of different bits of common sense? See if you can buy the bit that you want and what will you give in exchange?

The Horned Animals' Party

All the horned animals decided to have a party but other animals could not go unless they had horns. The dog and the cat wanted to go very badly so they got busy, killed a goat and took off the horns. Bro' Dog was to have the horns half of the night and then tie them on to Bro' Puss. So Dog took his turn but after he was in the party he didn't give Puss a thought. You know once you start singing and dancing you don't think of anything else. After the time when he was supposed to come out Puss got near the door and started to holler 'Bro' Dog, Bro' Dog' and Bro' Dog paid no heed. And Bro' Cattle who was the boss of the party came to the door and said – and he was really angry – 'Go away, go away. There is no dog in here.' Well Bro' Puss got really angry. Then Bro' Dog himself came out and hushed Bro' Puss. But Bro' Puss was so mad he kept on shouting. Bro' Cattle came out again and said 'Maybe Bro' Dog is in here' and began to search until they discovered Bro' Dog and they tore off his ears and started to beat him. Bro' Dog hollered and rushed out. He met Bro' Puss and began to fight with him. And Bro' Puss scratched Bro' Dog on the lip.

If you look at the corner of a dog's mouth it looks raw. That's why. And that's why a dog and a cat can never agree.

Themes

Fighting and arguing.

Getting your own back.

Going where you shouldn't go and the consequences.

Baby in the Crib

John stole a pig from Old Marsa. He was on the way home with him and Old Marsa seen him. After John got home he saw Old Marsa coming down to the house. So he put the pig in a cradle they use to rock the babies and he covered him up. When Old Marsa came in, John was sitting there rocking him.

Old Marsa said 'What's the matter with that baby, John?'

'The baby got the measles.'

'I want to see him.'

John said, 'Well you can't. The doctor said if you uncover him the measles will go back in and kill him.'

So his Old Marsa said, 'I still want to see him.' He reached to uncover him.

John said, 'If that baby is turned into a pig now don't blame me.'

Themes

This can introduce the theme of slavery and the history of slavery, and how people learnt to survive.

How oppressed people might describe the worst possible lives through humour.

The theme of trickery. Playing tricks.

No Tracks Coming Back

You know Brer Rabbit said to be the wisest animal in the forest. So Brer Rabbit was walking along one day when Brer Fox came along. 'Say, Brer Rabbit, ain't you going to the big meeting? Everybody goin'. 'Zat so', said Brer Rabbit, 'sure I'm going.' Pretty soon he sees hundreds of footprints and all goin in de sam direction. Den he see dey all rabbit tracks. 'Mmmmm', says Brer Rabbit, 'all dem tracks goin dat way, an not a single one coming dis way. Dat ain't no place fo me.'

Themes

Again the theme of saving yourself, being cautious.

The moral is distanced by making an animal the protagonist.

The story can be played as it is told.

Pairs make up stories of one person trying to entice another.

Such stories could be used for work about keeping safe, not going with strangers.

Arab stories

Djuba Fries Quail (Egypt)

One day two friends called on Djuba. He was frying quails and the two friends watched. 'This dish lacks salt', said one after he had picked the bird out of the pan and tasted it. 'Not enough vinegar', said the second friend as he picked up the second quail. Djuba picked up the last quail. 'What does it matter', he said, 'because now the dish lacks quails?'

Themes

Trickery

How laughter can ease tension.

The Woodcutter without Brains (Morocco)

Two woodcutters were out walking when they saw lion tracks on the road. 'There must be a lion about', said one, 'What shall we do?' said the other. 'Let's go on and do what we have to do!' said the first woodcutter. So they went on along the path and collected their firewood. When it was time to go back the first man said, 'Let's take a different way home, in Allah's name!' 'No this way is shorter', said his friend. The first man said, 'I saw lion's tracks on the path, I shan't return that way.' And he took the higher path up the rocky mountain.

The second woodcutter returned the same way as he had come. When he got to the place where he saw the lion tracks there was the lion himself. 'Peace, Uncle Lion', said the man. 'Peace, son of Adam', said the lion. 'What are you doing here?' said the man. 'I am sick', said the lion, 'and I need the brain from the head of a man to cure me.' 'Listen, O lion', said the man, 'for what I am about to tell you is the truth. I am a brainless fellow. If I had any brain I wouldn't have returned this way. The one with the brains is up on the higher path behind the rocks.' 'God grant you happiness', said the lion and began to climb the mountain.

Themes

Taking chances

Trickery

When One Man Has Two Wives (Syria)

A man had two wives and they both loved him, though one was young and the other old. Whenever the man lay down to sleep with his head on his young wife's knees she would pluck the white hairs from his head so he would appear young like herself. And whenever he rested his head in his older wife's lap she would pluck out the black hairs from his head so he should be white haired like herself. And it was not long before the man was bald. And that is the origin of the saying 'Between Hannah and Bannah vanished are our beards.'

Theme

Trying to be all things to everybody

The Cat Who Went to Mecca (Syria)

Once long ago, the King of the Cats went on a pilgrimage to Mecca. When he returned the King of the Mice felt he should pay him the traditional visit of congratulations for his safe return as a Hajji or pilgrim. The mice were not convinced. 'This cat is our enemy. How can we go near him in safety?' The King explained, 'Now the cat has been to Mecca he is no longer free to do what he did before. He plays all day long from dawn to sunset.' The mice were not convinced. 'You go, we'll wait here.' So the King of the Mice left his hole and looked around. There sat the King of the Cats praying. But no sooner had the King of the Cats caught sight of the King of the Mice than he sprang and but for God the Preserver he would have bitten the mouse's tail right off. The King of the Mice jumped back into his hole, and rejoined his subjects. 'How is the King of the Cats after his pilgrimage?' they said. 'Has he changed for the better?' 'Never mind the pilgrimage' said the King of the Mice. 'He may pray like a Hajji but he still pounces like a cat.'

End in the way of Arab storytellers:

Mulberry, mulberry
Here ends my story

With the final wish of all tellers of tales:

We left them happy, and back we came.
May Allah make your life the same!

Asian stories

One Man's Pleasure (an Urdu story)

A man from Kabul in Afghanistan once went to visit India.

One day he was walking down an Indian street when he came to a sweetmeat shop selling all sorts of wonderful sweets of all sizes, shapes and colours.

He knew only a few words of Hindustani. He went up to the sweet seller and pointed out a delicious pile of sweets. The vendor thought he was asking the name of the sweet so he said 'Khaja'. The word means both sweets and 'eat it up'. The man from Kabul knew only the second meaning so he grabbed a handful of sweets and ate them all up.

The vendor of sweets asked the man to pay for the sweets. But the visitor didn't understand what he was saying and wandered away.

The angry vendor complained to the police who came and arrested the man from Kabul. The chief officer ordered that his head should be shaved clean and covered with tar and that he should be mounted on a donkey and chased out of town on a procession to the sound of drums so that everyone should know that is how a lawbreaker is punished in that part of the world.

This was thought to be a brutal punishment in India but the man from Kabul thought it was fun. He felt charmed and honoured as he processed through the streets. He was the centre of attention.

On his return to Afghanistan people asked him about his trip to India. He answered, 'It is a wonderful country, and a very rich country. You get everything for nothing there. You go to a shop, point to a pile of sweets and they tell you to take all you want and eat it.

'Then the police come with drums, give you a shave, dye your hair with hair dye, give you a nice donkey to ride through the town to the accompaniment of lovely Indian music.

'And all for nothing. Wonderful country, kind hosts and beautiful people.'

Themes

A stranger in a different country. The difficulties of communication when you don't understand the language. Cultural differences and misunderstandings which can be humiliation for one person and a matter of humour for another.

The story could be played as it is told, care being taken to contain the episode where the man from Kabul is run out of town.

Scenes from the story could be explored, e.g. how to communicate when you don't know the language.

Ideas from the story could be developed in the contexts

of the lives of people in the group. For example, going on holiday to a different country or when aspects of a culture are misunderstood and the consequences of this which may be more serious than in this story.

A Drum (a Hindi story)

There was once a poor woman who had only one son. She worked hard cleaning houses and received grain in return for her work.

One day as she went to market to sell the grain she asked her son what he wanted from the market. 'A drum, mother, I'd like a drum.'

The mother went to market to sell her grain and buy food for her and her son. She knew she wouldn't have enough money to buy food and a drum for her son and she felt sad.

On the way home from market she saw a beautiful piece of wood on the road so she brought it home as a present for her son.

The son carried the piece of wood when he went out to play. He saw an old woman who was trying to light her stove but the fire was not catching so the boy offered her his piece of wood to start her fire. The old woman was very pleased. She lit her fire, baked some bread and gave a piece to the boy.

He took the bread and walked on until he met a potter's wife whose child was crying. The boy asked the mother why the child was crying and she said she had no food for the child. The boy gave her his piece of bread. The potter's wife was grateful to the boy and gave him one of her pots.

The boy walked on until he came to a river where he saw a washerman and his wife quarrelling. The boy asked them why they were fighting. The washerman said that his wife had broken the only pot they had. 'Now I've nothing to boil the clothes in before I wash them.' The boy said, 'Here, don't quarrel. Take this pot and use it.' The washerman was very happy and gave the boy a coat.

The boy walked on. Then he met a man on a bridge, shivering without his shirt. The boy asked him what had happened. He said he had been robbed of all his possessions, even his shirt. 'Don't worry,' said the boy. 'You shall have this coat.' The man was so grateful that he gave the boy a horse.

The boy took the horse and very soon met a wedding party with the musicians, the bridegroom and his family. But they were sitting under a tree looking very miserable. The boy asked them what was wrong.

The bridegroom's father said that they were waiting for the man to bring a horse so they could go in the wedding procession. 'The bridegroom can't arrive on foot and we'll miss the auspicious hour for the wedding.'

So the boy offered them his horse and they were delighted.

When the bridegroom asked him what he could do in return the boy said, 'You can give me something. That drum the musician is carrying.'

The bridegroom asked the musician who gave the drum gladly as he knew he would be well paid by the bridegroom.

The boy rushed home to tell his mother that he had a drum and he told her the whole story, beginning with the piece of wood she gave him.

Themes

Parents doing the best they can but keeping their priorities of care for the child. For example, food must come before the drum.

The meaning of a gift. Giving something to express love and care for a person.

Reciprocity. Giving and getting back, not by right but as a communication.

Negotiating communication.

Each of the small meetings within the story can be played as the sequence builds to the end where the needs of everybody in the story are met by communication and negotiation

The meaning of gifts can be very important for people who have experienced difficult attachments to people and who trust objects more than people. This story shows the satisfaction of giving based on equality rather than giving or getting as a means of exerting power.

Playing scenes from the story can give participants skills in giving and receiving gifts negotiated on the basis of equality between people.

5

Drama for people with learning disabilities

Drama can be an excellent way of developing self esteem with groups of children and adults with learning disabilities both as a medium to develop creative expression and as a way of learning tasks and skills.

PREPARATION

It is important to understand the aims and objectives of the school, day centre or institute which organises the programme of work/meetings so that the drama group can integrate in some way with the general programme. The aims and work of the drama group should be shared with other staff and potential group members so that the group are not marginalised but part of the mainstream activities. Open communication can help others understand drama activity and its importance for healing and perhaps alleviate the anxiety some people have about what goes on in drama.

STARTING THE GROUP

Information about the group
The leader should find out as much as possible about the members of the group especially their level of functioning. This includes chronological age and developmental level including intellectual, social and emotional understanding. A clear knowledge will help the group leader offer drama material which will be appropriate and safe for the skill level of the group.

This information about the group should be a base for beginning the work but not limit the expectations of the leader. The creative force of drama can often empower individuals and as they gain self confidence they feel able to show skills and imaginative ideas which may have lain hidden because they were uncertain about whether their contribution would be valued. But, on the other hand, there is nothing more damaging for the group and leader than to begin with ideas and play beyond the understanding and competence of the group.

Selection of the group

Selection of group members is important and can determine the content of much of the work. Many groups have members who are functioning socially at a level where they are not yet able to separate self from the object world outside themselves. Their functioning will be as a set of individuals who happen to be together. Most time will be spent with the whole group doing the same thing. With small groups working on different projects, each group will need a helper to structure the work.

If there is a more sophisticated level of social interaction, then the group may be more able to work in small groups without a helper and share ideas between themselves. They may be able to develop their own ideas beyond imitation and repetition. Such a group can become more boisterous because the social skills may be at a basic level and sharing could cause fighting and tears. This can be part of a positive social skills training and is not necessarily a sign of failed group communication. Size of group and/or number of helpers is important if the group are learning social skills at a basic level because each difficulty must be resolved as it happens and this is labour intensive.

Objectives

Sometimes the chaos can seem threatening to the leader so clear preparation, careful structure and simple objectives are important. Change can then be perceived by the group and the leader and self esteem begins to emerge for individuals, the group and the leader.

A careful step-by-step approach with clear objectives understood by everybody gives boundaries to the group and the leader and this in turn limits the chaos because everybody knows what is acceptable to the group.

Boundaries

The rules and boundaries of care for each other will have been discussed and agreed as part of the contract for the group before starting the sessions. A group with learning disabilities need boundaries of social interaction to be made explicit. Rules such as no hitting, swearing, running off out of the room, need to be agreed. Then rules about talking and listening, for example: group members must look and listen to the person talking and take turns not all talking at once. If the rules are agreed at the beginning then chaos will be less and easier to control by reference to the rules.

Models of drama work

Decisions about whether the group will work through the Creative-Expressive model or the Tasks and Skills model (described in Chapter 1) will be determined by the needs of the organisation, the needs of the group and where the group fit into the general programme for those particular individuals.

At a day centre for adults, for example, the focus for the group may be Creative-Expressive to develop the imaginative dramatic skills of the participants through movement, puppet work, play and improvisation.

In an education unit for adolescents the focus of the group may be task based. The purpose of such a group may be to empower individuals to learn body boundaries as part of a general sex education programme. This could be accomplished through the use of storytelling, movement, puppets and role play.

IDEAS FOR A CREATIVE-EXPRESSIVE GROUP

Body work

A way of beginning a drama group with people with learning difficulties is to introduce embodiment play recalling early stages of physical movement. This is a good way to establish relationship play and an awareness of body parts and the way the body moves.

These activities begin on the floor and end there: the safe place from which to explore the world.

Appropriate clothes for moving around the floor and other movement activities should be worn. It is important to explain this when group rules are being prepared because there is nothing worse than playing in the wrong kind of clothes and feeling self conscious. This can happen if discussion about clothes is not made explicit.

Veronica Sherbourne (1990) describes three types of relationship play which can be established through developmental movement. These are: caring relationships, shared relationships and 'against' relationships. All these ways of being can be enacted through movement. If the group members are able to share and help each other then all the play can be experienced amongst themselves. If this is too complicated because of the level of learning difficulties then helpers will be needed to share in the play.

Caring relationships can be experienced through movement play such as rolling and sliding.

Rolling and sliding

Work with a partner/helper.

Leader shows you how to roll in a sequential way from the hip, shoulder or knee with the rest of the body following with a twist of the trunk.

With the support of your partner begin to roll over in that way. Perhaps your partner needs to help with a gentle push to start the roll.

When you have learnt this, then rolling becomes fluent and you can roll really fast. Your partner must make sure you don't bump into anyone else as you roll.

Rolling down your partner

With a partner.

One of you sits with legs straight.

Your partner lies across your knees and rolls down to your ankles and back again.

A bumpier ride but a lot of fun.

Rolling your partner

Roll your partner from side to side.

Do this gently without hurting your partner.

Don't roll too fast.

Sliding

Sliding can be fun. Pull your partner by the ankles across a slippery floor.

Again, care of the other person is part of the learning as well as the sense of freedom sliding brings.

Shared relationships, which require a level of trust between two people, can include simple activities such as 'rowing a boat'.

Rowing

Sit on the floor facing your partner. Hold hands and pretend to row backwards and forwards as though you were in a boat.

For older people: balance your partner as you rise from the ground by holding hands and judging the distance between you. Move from the floor to standing position and back to sitting, keeping the balance right. This requires concentration and skill.

'Against' relationships

'Against' relationships are a way to help people to test and control their strength against a partner.

Back-to-back push

Partners sit back to back with knees bent.

Both dig their heels into the ground.

They place hands flat on the floor behind.

Then they push backwards to see how strong they are.

This can be a way of testing strength which is not a question of winning.

Testing doesn't need to have one winner, both can be strong at a certain point.

There are many variations of back-to-back games which can be developed according to the skill and control of the group.

Feelings aroused in developmental body work

There is a powerful emotional experience in re-creating developmental movement play as many people remember their first experiences of movement as a baby. This can evoke happy or sad memories depending on the early experiences of childhood and such play can be of value in any group as a way of re-experiencing early childhood.

People with learning difficulties can be particularly vulnerable so it is important for helpers and leaders not to force body boundaries for this may make individuals **more** vulnerable to abuse. Respect and regard for the other person's body boundaries is central to this work.

The body in space
From developmental movement the group can explore the space around their bodies and ways of using and experiencing that space.

Space walk
Talk the group through this experience.

> Walk around the space in the room and feel the space around you as you move through the room.

> Explore the space around you, feel it against your body, your neck, shoulders, back, legs, on the top of your head, inside your mouth.

> Feel the shape of your body as you move around the room.

> As you walk, imagine that the space around you is touching you; your face, neck, the whole of your body.

From this space walk the group can imagine different physical environments to experience such as:

the inside of a balloon,

inside a glass ball depicting a snowstorm,

a huge vat of golden treacle.

Snail shell
Partners

> Together find a space in the room where you feel safe. One of you curls up on the floor and imagines you are a snail, curled up safe and warm in your shell. The partner has to persuade you to come out of your shell and enjoy the world.

This can be done verbally or non-verbally according to the skill of the group but the persuasion has to be gentle and quiet.

If it is too cosy and safe in the shell then the snail can stay there and not come out.

What will make your partner come out of the shell? Ice-cream? TV? Money? Friends? A nice day out? No school?

Partners change over.

Then perhaps everybody in the group curls up in a shell and feels safe and warm curled round in it.

This can end a session with quiet and safety before everybody is asked to stretch out of the shell and slowly uncurl, sit up and look around the room.

Improvisation

For a group with limited skill at working together, improvisation can begin with storytelling from the leader and the whole group imitating the action of the story as it is being told.

It is important to begin storytelling about events and places known to the group like a visit to the local café, or a day out at the theme park. Any kind of journey which has significance for the group is a good starting point.

The leader begins the story, perhaps describing the journey to school or a walk to the park. The group act the journey as the leader describes events: for example, the group have to cross a busy road, or they see an air balloon floating overhead. The leader could describe playing in the park then, tired and happy, everybody goes back to school for tea.

This kind of play can be introduced by games and songs such as:

Here we go round the mulberry bush,
    the mulberry bush, the mulberry bush,
Here we go round the mulberry bush,
    on a cold and frosty morning.
This is the way we wash our clothes,
    wash our clothes, wash our clothes,
This is the way we wash our clothes
    on a cold and frosty morning.

Then actions can be amended to the skill and sophistication of the group:

This is the way we plait our hair . . .

This is the way we lace our trainers . . .

This is the way we rock and roll . . .

The aim of the game is to share observations of how we do physical tasks and to get ideas of things to do from the group. Another way of introducing such play can be from reading a story which the group can play. A good story of this kind is *In a Minute* by Tony Bradman and Eileen Browne about a family outing to the playground which is delayed as the parents get things ready and chat to people they meet, constantly telling the children, 'We'll be with you in a minute.'

After reading the story and showing the pictures the group leader could take appropriate parts of the journey to the playground for the group to act out. The repetitious line, 'We'll be with you in a minute,' makes a good chorus for the whole group to chant.

If the group can separate into two smaller groups which work separately, then some activities from the story can be shown by one group and the rest of the story by the other group. It is still important for the leader to narrate and keep the structure of the story for the safety and sense of achievement of the group.

Games with rules

Games with rules can be too complex for many groups with learning difficulties but some games can be appropriate for some people. The group must be at the stage of learning when members are socially aware of other people and understand that individuals can have different roles in a game. The difficulties arise if this concept is not grasped. However, there are some games of imitation where everybody in the group must imitate the leader and these can be tried with many groups.

Crooked Path

This is an American Indian game from the Plains, Woodlands and Northwest Coastal tribes. This can be played indoors or outdoors.

The leader makes up a simple song as she leads the line of players. One Plains Tribe song is,

Follow the leader, follow him well,
What he'll do next, no one can tell.

As the leader walks she makes steps, jumps or imitates
the movements of birds and animals and the group has
to imitate the movements.

Those who can't imitate the movements drop out of
the line.

It is important to keep the rhythm of the song and
make the movements rhythmic as the line and the
game progresses.

Danger Signal

This is another game from the same Indian tribes and is a
hiding game so there need to be hiding places indoors if played
inside.

Players are told to spread out and listen for danger
signals like those of animals and birds and human
warning whistles.

Sounds like the warning bark of a dog or the hoot of
an owl.

If they hear a warning cry from the leader, the group
freeze, if they are hidden or silently take cover.

Between warning whistles the group are to keep on the
move silently, finding cover as best they can.

The test is to see how well people in the group can stay still
and hidden and how silently they can creep around before they
hear the danger signal.

Can you do things together?

This game is about sharing activities either with a partner or
the whole group depending on the skill of the players. Change
the instructions to suit.

Can you skip with your partner?

Can you crawl through a hoop without letting go of
your partner's hand?

Can you be very small with your partner?

Can you move around the room back to back with
your partner?

Can you sit face to face with your partner and row a
boat?

Can you roll your partner over like a log?

Can you stand your 'log' up like a telephone pole?

Can you walk through a field of jelly with your
partner?

Can you swim through Ghostbusters' Slime with your
partner?

Frozen tag

This is a form of tag when there are several players
who are 'freezers'.

The rest of the group are chased by the freezers and
when caught they stay frozen with an arm extended or
legs in a stride position.

As the players run round they can unfreeze a person
by crawling under their legs or by shaking their hand.

All these games and activities can help the group make connections with each other according to their capacity to cope with
social relationships.

Develop the work slowly. Simple pleasures and activities can
bring great pleasure and help individuals feel they have something to offer.

TASK BASED GROUP

Many tasks can be undertaken in a drama group and various
drama ways of working can be used to reinforce information
and help the group learn appropriate skills through practice
in one form or another. People with learning difficulties can
often use play with toys and puppets and learn well through
projected play rather than direct role play. Repetition is important when new ways of social interaction are being taught so
it is important not to have too many learning objectives.

EXAMPLE

One of the most important issues for those with learning difficulties is to develop an awareness of body boundaries and so
help protect themselves from abuse.

Body boundaries

The issues of such a group would be:

1 to develop an awareness of the body;

2 the naming of body parts;

3 from the initial naming would be the definition of private parts.

'Good' touches and 'bad' touches

1 The next stage would be to help the group understand that everybody has a right to say 'no' to body touch;

2 that there are 'good' touches and 'bad' touches;

3 finally who to tell if somebody gives you a 'bad' touch.

This might be accomplished in ten group sessions but could take longer with some groups who might need more reinforcement of information. Play and drama would be the central mode of working but direct information with illustrations would also be part of the group learning. Both modes of working would operate together during each session. Talk reinforced by play and play reinforced by talk.

AWARENESS OF THE BODY

Developmental movement can be a good beginning. It can lead through relationship play, as described in this chapter (page 77). The work on 'against' relationships can also help the leader assess who has the capacity to exert an appropriate amount of body strength and who is compliant and allows invasion of personal body space.

Naming of body parts

There are many songs and games which name body parts and can be used. I like the book *Freckly Feet and Itchy Knees* by Michael Rosen (1990) which contains simple rhymes about noses, hands, feet, eyes, knees and finally bellies. The rhymes are repetitive and jolly and the illustrations funny. The rhymes can be used for movement games, improvisation or just listening, looking and enjoying.

Talking points could be:

hands that smack,

hands that stroke,

hands that point,

hands that poke.

As the book ends on bellies, then bottoms seem to be the next phase.

GOOD TOUCH AND BAD TOUCH

Play around 'good' touch and 'bad' touch can begin with such touches as:

pushing, being tickled too hard, pinching, pushing

before defining private zones of the body; before defining sexual molestation.

This work needs to be taught and played, setting up simple enactments, perhaps with puppets or using drawing.

Good illustrations and appropriate literature help reinforcement.

Puppet play

Puppet play can be introduced and the group can make up stories showing good and bad touches. I use a crocodile puppet, a puppet of a boxer with punching arms, a mouse and rabbit puppet to define good touches and bad touches and set up simple scenes about body boundaries and how to keep them. The group can make up their own stories and often describe incidents which have happened to be played out with the puppets.

Books like *It's My Body* (1984) can give ideas for play and *Where Do I Come From* (1973) can help teach information about the body.

Such a programme would be an integrated part of a larger learning programme so that discussion would be carried on outside the group. Information about body functions can cause some anxiety for the group so time is needed for repetition and absorption of the ideas and information. Adolescents with learning difficulties are often afraid to appear ignorant about sexual matters and need to feel confident; play and enactments give confidence by allowing strategies to be tried out in the safety of the drama group. Other tasks appropriate for drama could be learning to share with other people, fighting and bullying.

I use a book called *What Feels Best* (1988) which describes how a kangaroo learns to be sociable. The book describes behaviour which is selfish and then strategies to be kind to others.

Each of the descriptions could be used as a basis for a simple enactment or a sculpt of the scene to show to the rest of the group.

DESCRIPTION OF A CREATIVE-EXPRESSIVE GROUP

WORK WITH A GROUP OF AUTISTIC ADOLESCENTS

This is a description of some group work undertaken by myself and Hank Gullickx, another dramatherapist, with two groups of adolescents living in a small residential home in the Netherlands. The home is for those people with autism who have good possibilities to develop emotionally, socially and cognitively. There were three groups living in the house. Members of a group were selected as being at about the same level of social, emotional and cognitive functioning, not by chronological age.

The aim of the work at the house was to develop the maximum social independence for each individual and the method of treatment was through intensive individual and group therapy. Hank and I worked with two groups who displayed many of the classic features described by the American child psychiatrist, Leo Kanner, when he made his initial description of the autistic syndrome in 1943 (see L. Wing (1976)):

a profound withdrawal from contact with people, an obsessive desire for the preservation of sameness, a skilful and even affectionate relationship to objects,

mutism, or the kind of language that does not seem intended to serve inter-personal communication.

The first group we worked with had not yet developed much social behaviour but were concerned with making sense of their own experience in isolation. They had few spontaneous reactions and little social talk.

At the beginning of the work there were five males in the group aged from 13 to 25 years. During the work one male left and two females joined the group.

With this group our aims were to use the Creative-Expressive model to explore the healthy aspects of the group. We tried to develop more individual body awareness and encourage the beginning of social interaction.

The second group were more involved with social behaviour but had limited ways of expressing feelings towards each other. There were four males and two females in this group aged from 13 to 23.

With the second group we were to try to develop the social contacts between members and find more options for group members to express their feelings towards each other. The work with both groups in the initial phase consisted of games and activities through which we could get to know the group, find out ways to develop drama and also discover what activities, noises, etc., produced anxiety.

We learnt a great deal about the group members during this observation time. Every person had marked obsessional or idiosyncratic behaviour and there were also some common behaviours of this kind. For example, fascination with time, telling the time, looking at the face of a watch, anxiety about certain fixed times. This was common to every group member. One person worried about the distinction between 'I must do' and 'I may do'. He was unable to do what he 'must' do but could do what he 'may' do. So often the question came, 'Must I do it?' Obsessional personal interests centred around such subjects as pop music, prehistoric life, lorries, computers.

Our initial work with the group centred round making circles and singing and counting games and these soon became another ritual but at the beginning and ending of the session made for comfort and security and signified beginnings and endings to make boundaries for everybody.

The first group were easier to work with in the beginning because their social interaction was limited so there was little conflict in the group. We had to play together with everybody in the group doing the same thing as we were a group of individuals with little social contact so it was difficult for one person to take a different role from the others and use it in the group.

We concentrated on games to develop physical dexterity, using ropes and wool for jumping and making complex mazes. We used rhythmic walks, jumping and hopping, with rhymes and rhythms to stimulate responses.

Gradually social contact developed in the group and this

brought behaviour conflicts between the physically assertive and the non-assertive. We went back to developmental movement and played some 'against' pushing kind of game to allow contained physical conflict.

Imaginative play through improvisation proved to be about imitation and limited observation which lacked individual development. The group were happiest imitating Hank or me. Hank began to structure the improvisations so that we started together but at a certain moment the group were left to develop their own ideas and invent things for themselves. Progress was slow but ideas began to emerge.

The improvised play centred around events shared by the group, such as bus trips and other journeys. Hank had to ask a lot of questions to encourage individual ideas.

The second group were more difficult to work with in the beginning. They were socially aware of each other but couldn't negotiate the communication. There were constantly exploding situations with shifting relationships and aggressive outbursts. As the work progressed relationships became more settled in the group. When people are becoming aware of their need for social communication a drama group is a good learning place but there is still much anxiety and fear of failure for the individual and this must be contained within the structure of the group.

We began and ended the sessions with simple circle games but even these games became a complex activity full of social decisions about whose hand could be held at a given moment. It did give Hank and me an indication at the beginning of the session what conflicts and alliances were around and what might have happened in the interval since meeting last.

We concentrated on imaginative play with this group and they developed more skilful improvisations than the first group. We played 'animals' in groups, how they reacted to each other and to humans and the way they showed feelings such as anger and fear. These improvisations became metaphors of the group's situation which could be safely explored through the lives of other creatures.

We also worked on human movement that showed feelings. Simple play about walking happy, walking angry, what do angry feet look like?, what do waiting feet look like?, and so on. This group were more skilful at playing games and could understand simple rules in a social game. In the summer we developed quite complex variations on 'tag', using play equipment in the garden.

Both groups played and developed healthy aspects of their creativity and enjoyed the freedom to play. The first group gained pleasure in their individual skill in play and the second group learnt to play together and negotiate how to do this without always resorting to anger.

For those who have learning difficulties of whatever kind much time is spent by those who care in exhorting them to be responsible and sometimes this external pressure to achieve some kind of independence makes people with learning difficulties afraid to play and have fun.

In drama, players can get in touch with their capacity to play and it is always surprising how much independence can be learnt through play and how much skill in social interaction has to be achieved if the group are to play together.

6

Drama for people with physical disabilities

REASON FOR FORMING A GROUP

There are many reasons why a group of people who have some physical disability should meet together. It can be to share information, help and support, for re-affirmation and self advocacy or for pleasure and relaxation in each other's company. It might be that the group is part of school activity or could be, for example, a group which I occasionally work with who are diabetic young people. They meet with health professionals to exchange information about their condition but also to give support to each other and have fun together. For facilitators to be effective for such groups, they must either share the disability of the group and/or be able to offer some expertise which the group have agreed they want. It is important to listen to the group and be able to offer drama skills which meet their needs rather than an attitude of meeting a group with a little package of 'games and play for the hearing impaired, or play for the partially sighted'. I am often asked to give suggestions in that way without regard for the group process and how the group see their function and reason for being together. Clearly there are appropriate activities according to the physical capacity of the group but what is processed is determined by its members. I do not intend in this chapter to offer packages for disabilities but suggest activities which may interest or focus a group who want to share time together.

CREATIVE-EXPRESSIVE GROUP

Many groups want to explore their own creativity and the healthy aspects of themselves to develop their self esteem. The facilitator can offer themes of play and dramatic methods which emphasise the skill of the group.

The suggestions offered below can be used with a variety of groups who can choose what is appropriate for them and what they would like to do. I have worked with partially-sighted and blind children who wanted to take photographs because they liked the process of working the camera with direction about where to point it. Play with make-up can be fun even if you can't see the result and the vibrations created by sound and music can be exciting for those with auditory difficulties.

RELAXATION THROUGH GUIDED IMAGERY

Relaxation using imagery is a good way to stimulate the imagination and become aware of the body.

Time travel

Sit in a comfortable position which you can keep for some minutes. Close your eyes.

Be aware of your breathing, in and out.

Feel your breath as it moves in and out of your nostrils.

Let all your thoughts go out of your mind as your breath flows out.

Imagine that you are walking out of the room and there outside the door is a strange looking Time Machine.

You look at it, walk round it, look for the way in and then climb into the machine.

What colour is it? What is the machine made of? How easy is it to enter?

Look for the controls.

Find the information about time and choose a time and world you wish to travel to.

Is it the past or the future?

Close the door of the machine, press the controls and fly to your chosen place and time.

You arrive, step out of the machine and begin to explore this place and time.

Who is there, what is the place like, what do people do, what do they eat?

Talk with them.

How do they greet you?

Now it is time to go back to the Time Machine.

Say goodbye to the people or creatures you have met.

Ask for a sentence or a greeting or a saying which you can bring back with you to remember them by.

You return to the machine and set the dials for the present and this room.

Now you are flying back through time and now you are to land back in this room.

5–4–3–2–1– You land, step out of the machine, walk back into the room as the machine flies off on its own power.

You slowly stretch and open your eyes.

Ask the group to share their place and time and the saying or language which they brought back with them.

The safe place

Sit in a comfortable position, close your eyes and think about your breathing.

Feel the breath as it moves in and out of your nostrils.

As you breathe out your body gets more relaxed.

As you become relaxed, imagine you are moving in time and space and you are travelling to a place which is safe for you.

It may be a place of great beauty, hillside, country or by the sea. It may be a room or a space but somewhere where you feel safe.

Explore that space, the feel of the place, the colours, the smell.

How do you feel as you inhabit that space. What makes you feel so safe there?

Just be there and explore your contentment with it.

Now you are to leave that place and come back to the room;

but you can keep the feeling inside you which the place gave you as you return to the room.

Now open your eyes.

Draw the place or talk with your partner about how safe you felt and what you needed to get that feeling.

EMBODIMENT PLAY

For many disabled people who have experienced intrusive treatment on their bodies it is often a pleasure to experience sensory explorations of self and environment as a balance for those negative experiences.

I played with a boy of 5 who had endured two kidney transplants and he enjoyed making his kidney out of green sticky slime, stroking and shaping the material in a most tender way; saying goodbye to the part of himself he had lost.

Materials like clay and fluorescent Playdoh are pleasant materials just to touch and shape and enjoy and can be used for that experience by people who missed out on childhood experiences of sensory exploration.

Stage make-up

Make-up can be used as embodiment play to experiment with the feel of the make-up on the face and to change the face by the use of colour.

It is important when using make-up in this way to explain that we are not going to use the make-up to make representational faces like clowns or whatever but just to experiment with the colour, touch and texture of the material. In this way there is no ideal way to use the material, no sense of competition because everybody does just what they want and that is the aim.

It is important that each person paints her own face, it is not the objective to make up somebody else. Embodiment play is experiencing one's own body through the exploration of one's own senses.

Aqua-colour is a form of stage make-up useful for groups because it washes off with water and the colours are bright and vivid and easy to put on. The fluorescent colours are particularly dramatic. The easiest way to apply the colour is to wet the finger in water and slide it across the colour then apply to the face. Children's face paints are too difficult to manage and not bright enough to achieve satisfactory results. Give each member of the group two or three colours or share the whole lot around the group. Everybody has a cup of water to wet the fingers and a small mirror to see what happens.

The best way to use the colours for embodiment play is to suggest that the group imagine their faces as pieces of paper onto which they are just to make shapes like abstract pictures. The aim is to enjoy the smell, the colour and the feel and texture of the make-up on the face.

After each face 'painting' is completed, it is important to take a photograph so there is a lasting image of the face. An imprint can be made on kitchen paper pressed across the face which creates yet another image.

The make-up can then be washed off the face. Afterwards members of some groups will then enjoy helping each other to massage cream into the face which can feel comforting if it is what people want to do.

PLAY WITH OBJECTS

For those groups with limited mobility, play with objects, drawing, making objects with clay, etc., can be a way to stimulate drama and storymaking.

Animals

Use an assortment of miniature animals and miniature objects such as trees and small wooden buildings.

Work in groups, pairs or with individuals.

Select several miniatures and objects to create an environment in which to live and have adventures.

Describe the adventures to the rest of the group.

Family dolls

Use sets of miniature family dolls and objects.

Work in groups, pairs or with individuals.

Use the dolls to create a family scene and dramatise it for the rest of the group.

The perfect house

Use fluorescent Playdoh in a variety of colours.

Everybody makes an individual choice of colours with which to model 'the perfect house'.

When the model is finished describe the house and its environment to the rest of the group.

The village and the city

Negotiate with the rest of the group an environment for all the houses and decide what kind of place it has to be to accommodate all the models.

Decide what infra-structure is needed to maintain the community.

Is it a place where the needs of the group will be met?

Is it a social place or are individuals isolated from each other?

How does the community relate to the outside world?

Is the community varied or similar to the people in the group?

Is there easy access to the outside world or is the place contained?

It is interesting to create this world where everything is possible and it is a safe way for the group to explore their needs in relation to themselves, the group and the outside world. An insight into exploring what you say you want from the rest of the world, what is possible and what in the end you really need.

CREATING WORLDS

H.G. Wells in his book *Floor Games* (1911) described a play he developed with his two sons where the two boys each constructed from objects, boxes and miniature dolls and toys either 'marvellous islands' or 'cities'.

In 'marvellous islands' the floor was the ocean and each

child had places in the ocean where he could construct islands. When the islands were ready each child explored his brother's island and H.G. Wells constructed a commentary. People would be sent from one island to the other to find out about customs. In the game of 'cities' the boys built twin cities or cities with two quarters so each child was head of his city. Again the city was constructed and adventures were devised by the boys and their father.

Both these games can be adapted for groups and through the safety of these imaginative explorations the individual and the group can express their feelings about themselves and the rest of the world.

Lowenfeld's world technique
This is a therapeutic technique developed by Margaret Lowenfeld (1970) as a way of giving children a language through which to express themselves.

While this technique is used in therapy, the materials used can be adapted to a dramatic model and is of particular advantage to individuals who have limited mobility but can handle small objects and figures.

In this technique the materials used are:

a collection of miniature dolls;

a metal tray measuring 75 x 52 cm with a depth of 7 cm; the inside of the tray should be blue to give the impression of water;

sand, water (the tray is filled with sand to within an inch of the brim);

a box of materials such as plasticine, string, stones, paper.

Her catalogue of World objects includes figures to represent basic categories of

human beings, including adults, children, figures in uniforms representing occupations (some figures sitting, some standing);

animals, including wild and domestic animals;

countryside objects such as trees, fences, bridges and gates;

houses and other buildings;

means of transport – cars, trains, ships and boats and including a fire engine, police car, ambulance;

miscellaneous objects of topical interest such as figures from the current TV and film interests.

Use in drama

In drama these objects can be used by individuals in the group to explore worlds of their own making and show the picture they have made in the tray with as much explanation as they want to share.

The whole group could make a sculpt of that picture to enlarge the image at the direction of the picture maker.

Telling stories through the figures and their world

The World material can be used as a stimulus to make up stories and adventures which can be shared with the group who may want to act out the stories in the wider world of the drama room.

The material is stimulating yet structures the drama. This kind of play is greatly enjoyed and can continue endlessly because the individual and group have control over what they present and represent and while sharing the same objects they can create their own unique world.

This way of play can be used and adapted by many physically disabled groups, those who are hearing impaired can represent their worlds in pictures and make sculpts of those pictures for the whole group. They can represent stories and adventures through a series of images using different trays as three-dimensional models of stages of a story. Those with limited movement can spend many sessions creating their worlds in a small space and the material could be used to present a tactile world for those with partial sight.

One way Lowenfeld used the material was to show the child that the adults and children lived on opposite banks of a river and suggest that the task for child and therapist was to create a bridge between the adults and the children and then devise ways of crossing that bridge.

While the task of drama for special needs is not directly therapy this is a powerful image for those isolated by disability and can be used by the group to explore that gap and examine the isolation that disability may bring to the individual.

STORYMAKING

There are many potent stories which explore difference and sameness which are often an abiding theme for groups with disability. One such story is 'Children of Wax', an African story.

There was once a family whose children were made of wax. The mother and the father were flesh as everybody else but for some reason the children were made of wax. The parents were very sad and wondered if somebody had put a spell on them, but in spite of everything they loved their children dearly.

These wax children were very easy to love because they were well behaved and worked twice as hard as other children. They never fought with each other and always did as they were told.

All the difficulties with the children were because of being made of wax. Their parents couldn't make a fire too close to them and they could only work at night. If they worked in the day they would melt.

Their father made them a hut with no windows to keep them out of the sun and in the day when the sun shone the children stayed in their hut, but at night the children would come out of their hut and begin to work. They looked after the crops and cattle as other children did in the day.

Ngwabi, one of the wax children, was very sad about this. 'We can never know what the world is like because we see so little in the dark at night.'

His brothers and sisters understood what he said but they accepted their lot and there were advantages. After all, being wax they never felt pain as other children. But Ngwabi was still sad and dreamt of the world he imagined from his nights out of the hut. He dreamt of the hills, and the bush and the paths through the bush which he had never taken. He longed to be free to wander where he would.

As Ngwabi grew older his longing became stronger and stronger and one day he could contain himself no longer and when the sun was high in the sky he ran out of the hut into the light. The light was brighter than he had ever imagined and he was amazed. The other children were terrified and screamed for their brother. They tried to catch him as he ran out of the hut but he escaped and was gone down the path.

But before he had gone a few steps down the path the heat of the sun drew all the strength from his limbs and crying out to his brothers and sisters he fell to the ground and melted into a pool of wax. Inside the hut, afraid to leave the darkness the other children wept for their brother.

When night came the other children went to the path to the place where Ngwabi had fallen. They picked up the wax and went to a special place they all knew and loved. There, in that place, Ngwabi's sister made the wax into a bird. It was a beautiful bird with huge wings and for feathers the children put a covering of leaves onto the wings from a tree which grew in that special place. These leaves would protect the wings from the sun when it grew hot in the day.

After they had finished they told their parents what had happened and what they had done. They all kissed the wax model of the bird. They set the bird on a rock in front of the children's hut.

The children did no work that night, at dawn the children were in their hut peeping through a small crack in the wall. As the light came over the hill it touched the wax bird which seemed to glow with fire. As the sun rose over the fields the great bird suddenly beat its wings and flew into the air. It flew high into the air and circled over the children's hut. Soon it was gone and the children knew that their brother was happy at last.

There are many ways to work with this story and many resonances for those who feel their body is different or have to experience the consequences of their physical disability or illness.

One theme to explore might be to examine the contrasts between light and dark, heat and cool.

Light and dark, heat and cool

Write all the words associated with light and dark. In small groups share your feelings about light and dark.

In pairs, use your bodies without speaking to express images of hot and cool, light and dark.

Show the movement to the rest of the group.

Talk about what it felt like.

Listen to the leader telling the story, 'Children of Wax.'

Imagine you are one of the children of wax. Write words and short sentences or draw pictures to describe:

what you do and feel at night when you are working outside; and
in the day in your hut with no windows.

With your partner find one picture or sentence which is the most important for you.

Share these important drawings and sentences with the whole group.

Make a group collage with the drawings and sentences.

Talking about the story
Another way to work with the story might be to talk about the topsy-turvy life of the children.

Story to enactment
Another activity might be for the group to use themselves and objects in the room to make the imaginary transformation from the pile of wax into the protected bird who can fly, the wax protected by leaves from the tree which grows in the special place.

This is a powerful story for the physically disabled. It is important to explore the ideas expressed in the story in symbolic form and to explore as far as the group wish to go but to keep to the symbolic form of the story and use the story as the means of expressing what the group wishes to share. There are many stories which have resonances and can be researched by the leader or found by members of the group.

CASE HISTORY
Peter aged 5. Recovering from a Second Kidney Transplant. We played together for some months after Peter's second transplant. The play took place once a fortnight, an hour's session at each meeting. Toys and objects were provided by me and the themes of the play and drama provided by Peter with me as audiences/sympathetic listener.

This was a combination of drama and playtherapy. The therapeutic method is explained in detail in my book *Play Therapy with Abused Children* (1992).

Peter used the same play material each time we met and the themes he presented were symbolic expressions of his feelings about being ill and his feelings about his body and his dysfunctional kidney.

The objects he used were a variety of miniature monsters, tubs of green sticky slime, Playdoh and drawing materials. He played a series of stories about monsters swimming in a lake or sea of slime, being rescued/not being rescued, being pulled out of the sea which was very rough or drowning in the sea.

His other theme was about being lost in a maze, a ghostly maze and he told me a variety of stories about what it felt like being in the maze. He used this theme for drawing work and playing about being in the maze.

The third theme was his anger with his dysfunctional kidney and he used the slime to make models of the organ. We played a lot of games about telling this kidney to get organised and start working properly. This became a little dialogue between the two of us.

One of his stories of the maze

This is a maze, a ghostly maze and I stand at the beginning. The maze is made of lots of different colours which you see as you walk through. If you stop in the maze you turn into a vampire. If you stop in the green colour you turn into a vampire, if you stop in the red you become invisible, you turn into nothing.

You've got to go two times round this maze and you come out like a vampire. If you stop on the green the second time round you turn into another kind of monster. This happened yesterday just like on the news.

Peter used symbolic play to express his feelings about his illness and he felt safe with the structures and boundaries which we agreed before we started to play. In this safe place, outside 'real' time, with rules and boundaries he could make sense of his situation and accept what he couldn't change and have his rightful anger accepted by a listening adult.

SELF ADVOCACY GROUP

Tracking down oppression: some ideas of Augusto Boal

Groups of older people and adults might want to express some of their oppression as differently-abled people and a way might be to explore some of the ideas and theatre work of Boal. Some of the games and exercises Boal uses in preparatory work to create themes for his Forum Theatre could be explored by the group.

In Forum Theatre the audience are no longer spectators but both actors and spectators. There is no 'stage', actors and spectators are in the same space. The actors perform a scene about being oppressed and the spect-actors can suggest alternative ways that the oppressed person could take to solve her oppression. The spect-actor can take over the role in the play and the actors stay true to their role but improvise around the new plot created by the spect-actor. The Forum Theatre is led by a facilitator called the Joker who makes the rules and can make appropriate interventions.

Tracking down oppression through images

Ask each person to present an image, first of personal oppression and then of their oppressor.

Use sound, shape, symbol or caricature, share your image with the group, swap images and explore each other's image, feel it physically.

Boal describes this as the individual's experience and from this he moves to 'cores'.

Core

The individual presents an image of oppression as a still image, a story or an improvisation or just a sound.

The value of the image is that other people can identify with it.

Embryo

The 'cores' become an 'embryo' when they are redefined by a group who identify with them.

The 'core' becomes social, the singular plural.

Model

The 'embryo' in its social context. The model is the drama structure which takes into account the social factors which need to be changed.

Pilot and co-pilot

Pilot tells a story of a personal oppression.

Co-pilot listens, eyes closed.

They separate. Each one makes an image of the oppression and presents it to the other.

The pilot is asked to choose an image or an amalgam of both.

The group are asked if they identify with the image.

Those who do identify can try to add themselves to the image or to put other members of the group into the image to reinforce and shape it.

Ritual gesture

Boal describes these as the repeated physical patterns of daily life's oppressions.

1 A person shows a ritual action.

2 Others are invited to add to it.

3 When a group is involved, improvisation can begin.

The 'cores' and 'embryos' presented by the group can be generalised into themes and from those themes the group can choose one to develop into dramatic action.

Individual oppressions

The Boal method of theatre and therapy: some ideas from 'The Rainbow of Desire'

Boal describes the techniques for exploring individual oppression as Image Theatre.

He suggests that a new group should begin with a technique called the image of the images as this establishes a relationship between individual, singular problems and the collective problems a group is experiencing.

STAGE ONE: THE INDIVIDUAL IMAGES

Work in small groups of four to five people.

Each member to make an image of an actual oppression that is happening or could happen again.

The image can be expressed in a realistic, symbolic or metaphoric way but it must feel true.

The protagonist makes a sculpt of the image.

He puts the other players in whatever position he wants, either as oppressors or allies.

During this first stage, all members of the group construct their own individual images.

STAGE TWO: THE PARADE OF THE IMAGES

The small groups come together and each goes on the stage in turn to remake the images in front of everyone with each member adopting the role of the oppressed in the sculpt.

For each image, the director asks those watching for objective commentaries. People can make subjective commentaries, too, but the director must emphasise that these are individual ideas and not definitive.

Objective comments describe what everybody can see, e.g. a participant is seated with arms outstretched, while comments such as 'it appears to me' are subjective commentaries.

All the images are presented and the director underlines the factors common to all the images.

STAGE THREE: THE IMAGE OF THE IMAGES

The director then proposes that the large group form an image of all the images. This one image to contain the essential elements of all the others.

STAGE FOUR: THE DYNAMISATION

The director needs to verify the degree of connection between actor and image: the actor may identify with the images, or recognise the images and characters, or feel some resonance with the characters.

When these participant/image relationships have been verified then members of the large group move to three forms of dynamism.

First dynamisation: interior monologue
For about three minutes all the actors who have created the image utter, without self-interruption, the thoughts their characters are thinking at that particular moment. They speak as the characters, not as actors performing, about everything that comes into their heads.

Second dynamisation: dialogue
For a further three minutes the actors engage in dialogue with other characters in the image.

For these two dynamisations the actors must stay immobile so if they want to speak with a character who is invisible to them in the image, they must find a way to do so without moving.

Third dynamisation: desire in action
Very slowly, in slow motion, without speaking or making a sound, the actors move around trying to show their character's desires.

This is the first technique Boal describes for a group of people who want to explore personal self-affirmation through acknowledging the 'cops' in the head and the messages they give, both of which impede the individual from achieving 'the rainbow of desire'.

7

Drama with emotionally disturbed people

Five 12 year olds trooped into the room, sent to drama because they were not adapting to school and their behaviour was disruptive. One look at the space and they erupted, running around the room and swinging on a metal bar which ran across the roof space.

They were anxious and angry about the label 'disruptive' that hung around them, and had sent them to this group. They didn't know what was expected, felt punished, couldn't hold their feelings so exploded.

Ground rules

When order was restored we spent much of that first session together establishing ground rules for the group. Safety, both physical safety and emotional safety so that clear limits were defined. Respect for each other and me, confidentiality and support for each other in and out of the group, listening to each other, no put-downs, respect for the person, fair play. We established that the bar across the roof space could only be used if it was part of the drama activity and this became a sort of running gag as each week somebody constructed a story which used this bar. The game was to use the bar in different ways, never the same thing twice. How I praised their ingenuity and imagination as they swung across the bar escaping the dangerous swamps below, where crocodiles lay in wait, or sat on the bar as the gate to Heaven watching the affairs of mortals below! The bar became a metaphor for their own adaption to

106

school, how they could accommodate to the institution through the use of their imagination.

Boundaries are the most important safety mechanism for people who are anxious about their emotional control. Choice of material is also critical. Outbursts of anger from children and adults are often related to their lack of capacity to tolerate frustration so it is important initially to offer structured drama experiences which contain the group's anxiety.

For example, members of the school group were very skilled at visual observation and they constantly played the game of observing partners, remembering how they are sitting and what they are wearing, then closing their eyes while the partners change three things about their appearance, such as moving the watch to the other wrist or pulling one sock down a little. The game requires you to look at your partner and observe the changes. Everybody in the group was skilled at this game; it was an instant success so it became a group ritual. By the end of the sessions the skill level was exceptional. It was also a game which I couldn't do very well so there was warm laughter at my failure and pride at the group's skill.

As visual observation was a shared skill in the group I began to offer drama ideas which emphasised environment, how things looked, used masks, make-up, drawings, plans, maps to reinforce the skills the children obviously possessed.

Dealing with anger

As the group achieved confidence in this kind of drama, they began to cope with planning and processing drama ideas which required reflexion and negotiating within the group. Sometimes there were outbursts but, with carefully structured rules, members learnt to cope with each other and tolerate anger without resorting to hitting each other or taking flight from the room. It is important for the leader to have thought out ways of dealing with an individual in the group who may explode in anger. Groups should be small enough to be managed by the leader and helpers so no child or adult feels unsafe should anger erupt. There must be rules about what to do if someone chooses to leave the room or where to place a person having a temper tantrum. If all this is agreed, then when it happens, the level of anxiety of the group is contained because, as far as possible, what will happen is already known.

While some groups express their emotional distress through

anger, other groups may be depressed and seem unable to function. These groups also need boundaries to feel safe and the drama to be structured enough for people to dare to explore ideas.

Dealing with depression

I worked with a group of day patients in a psychiatric hospital who were depressed and anxious. We spent many weeks learning relaxation techniques before the group began to explore stories and to write small scenes, then to act the scenes. Much encouragement and reassurance were needed from me so that what was produced had value and meaning. Boundaries were about listening to each other, valuing feelings and ideas and acknowledging the effort required actually to be present in the group.

DRAMA MODEL FOR EMOTIONALLY DISTURBED CHILDREN AND ADULTS

Creative-Expressive model

The most appropriate model of work is a Creative-Expressive model to emphasise the creative, positive aspects of the group so that individuals can develop self esteem. This model can offer appropriate boundaries and safety for the group and enhance the self confidence and creativity of group members. The aim of the drama is to stimulate the imagination of the group through drama activities and encourage a sense of group solidarity through shared imaginative drama experiences.

It is necessary to select material which emphasises the health of the group and contains and helps to integrate group solidarity. Safety and containment are essential for those in emotional distress. It is all too easy to elicit inappropriate disclosures from group members about their personal pain but when this cannot be contained within the group, anxiety is heightened and creativity diminishes. The emphasis should always be on what the group can do together however small and that what each person does is good because it belongs to that person.

Warm-ups

For these groups, 'warm-ups' and beginnings are critical if the leader is to gain information about the feeling level of the group and to settle the group at a safe level for drama. For example, an adult group of day patients in a psychiatric hospital may need relaxation and guided imagery to help them begin to play. Adolescents with behaviour problems at school may need a vigorous game to explode energy before settling down to work with the group.

Sometimes it is clear from the way the warm-up has been experienced that the level of anxiety is so great that plans have to be revised and themes changed to keep safe boundaries for the group. The leader must be flexible enough to change themes or methods to contain the feelings of the moment.

IDEAS FOR GROUPS

Relaxation and visualisation

Before beginning any relaxation work make sure the room is safe from interruptions and be near enough to the door to control entry. Make sure everyone can lie on the floor or in a comfortable chair and feels safe. Some groups of older people prefer chairs to lying on the floor and women sometimes feel stress about lying on the floor if wearing a skirt or dress. There should always be discussion of appropriate clothing as part of the contract with the group before the first active session.

Beginning relaxation: group leader's talk

After the group have been prepared for relaxation, the leader begins to describe the process of relaxation.

Close your eyes, feel comfortable, begin to relax the body starting from the feet.

Concentrate on the feet. If your feet are tense then curl your toes and move the feet until the tension goes.

Stretch your feet then when you are ready, relax your feet. Feel how heavy your feet are. Now your feet are beginning to relax, they feel heavy.

Now let the mind go blank, take the thought away.

Now concentrate on your legs, feel the tension and where it is. Tense your legs then slowly relax lose the tension from the lower legs, knees, thighs until your legs feel heavy.

Now let the mind go blank, take the thought away.

Repeat this kind of instruction for the hips, back, chest, arms, neck and head, then focus on the heaviness of the whole body.

When the whole body is relaxed, concentrate on breathing.

Breathe in slowly and out slowly at an even pace.

Breathe in through the nose and out through the mouth.

The movement for quiet breathing should be felt at the centre of the body, mainly at the base of the ribs. Try to avoid shallow breathing from the shoulders and upper chest.

After a few minutes of quiet breathing ask the group to come out of relaxation.

Slowly open your eyes, stretch your body slowly like a cat and in your own time but slowly sit up and look around the room.

Don't move quickly.

As a leader you will soon create a dialogue which is soothing for the group. It is important that your voice is soothing and you give everybody enough time to relax each part of the body and to experience quiet breathing which is slower when the body is in a relaxed state.

Once the group have learnt to relax the body a little you can introduce some imagery. This may be useful at the beginning or at the end of a session according to the tensions of the group.

The Relaxing Cloud

Begin by lying on the floor, let your body relax, move around a little until you feel comfortable.

Now choose a spot on the ceiling to look at.

Let your eyes softly focus on that spot until the rest of the room just fades away.

Let your eyes get softer and softer until they close.

As your mind relaxes and floats along imagine you are lying outside watching clouds float by above you in the sky.

Watch them lazily and peacefully floating along.

Now find a place in your body which is very relaxed. Imagine that area surrounded by a warm fuzzy cloud of relaxation.

Let the area be supported inside the cloud, very relaxed, very warm.

Now let the cloud expand through other parts of you until your whole body is floating along inside this beautiful warm cloud.

And now it is time to come back to the people around you. Count down slowly until you are back in the room.

Physical games

It is very important to establish clear rules if games are to be used at the beginning of a session to re-establish the group identity, otherwise there will be heightened aggression instead of a relaxation of tension. However, I have found that it is often a point of honour with groups labelled 'aggressive' to keep rules in structured games.

The Raft of Medusa

The leader establishes the four corners of a raft in the middle of the room with a shoe or other object at each corner. The raft should be big enough to take all members of the group but not comfortably.

The group should be standing round the sides of the room. When the leader says 'go' all the group run to the raft and sit on it, then they have to begin to push other people off the raft just by using your shoulders and trunk.

No elbowing, scratching, biting, pinching, etc.

The people who are pushed off the raft become sharks in the ocean and can pull other people off the raft; they, too, become sharks until one person or no one is left on the raft.

While this may sound a very rough game, if the rules are made very explicit about how you can push people off the raft then it can be played.

Warn people to take off glasses, etc., and make it plain that nobody **has** to play this game.

This game is popular with children who in my experience have always kept the rules while groups of professional adults who have played this game on training courses often 'play dirty' but actually enjoy their moments of rebelliousness.

Tag

Any game of tag in all its varieties can be a good starter, for example,

Blob

One person is 'it'. The start of the 'blob'.

'It' chases around and each person tagged joins the 'blob' chasing the rest.

This continues until everybody is part of the 'blob'.

Shoe circle

Everybody sits in a circle.

A shoe is passed round the group from person to person without using hands and without dropping the shoe.

CHOOSING GAMES

Games like this can reconstitute the group each week and are useful for groups who find verbal contact difficult. Choosing a game which suits the energy level appropriate for everybody is a skill which has to be learnt by the leader. The Raft of Medusa may be great one week but a disaster ending in aggression the next. The leader has to judge when chasing games are appropriate and when other forms of play are more suitable. There are many books which describe games but be sure to understand the rules and the consequences of the actions of the games before offering them to a group. Find games which you feel comfortable playing and which don't raise your stress level or are too competitive.

WORK IN PAIRS

This kind of work can be suitable for those who find social communication difficult but can manage to play and develop drama with one other person.

This is equally effective with depressed people and those who are aggressive in their behaviour.

Mirror work

These are helpful ways for two people to observe themselves and their partner and experience how they move and look through their partner's imitations of their movements. It structures a task for people who are uncomfortable looking at themselves or others and helps control those who approach others inappropriately.

Looking in the mirror

Look carefully at your face in a mirror.

Look closely enough to get some information about yourself.

How do your eyes look into the mirror?

How are the lines on your forehead?

Do the corners of your mouth turn up or down?

What does your skin look like?

What does your face say about you?

Perhaps you could write a letter to your face or draw a picture.

Share this drawing or letter with a partner.

The person and the mirror

In twos.

Imagine one of you is a mirror, the other a person standing in front of the 'mirror'.

Stand face to face about a foot apart.

The person standing in front of the 'mirror' begins to move her body in slow motion using just the arms at first.

The 'mirror' copies the movements.

As the 'mirror' learns to copy movements the person can make more complicated movements using the whole body if possible.

Change roles often to experience both mirror and person.

Fancy dress party

This time imagine the person is dressing up to go to a fancy dress party and is putting on the costume.

Decide what you are to wear.

The mirror copies.

Getting up in the morning

Imagine you are getting up in the morning and getting ready to go out.

The mirror copies.

Try some variations.

Going out to visit the dentist.

Going out to a party.

Going out to buy a pet.

Going to a football match.

Famous person

You are a famous person living or dead.

Show that person to the mirror who copies and tries to guess who you are.

Statues

For those who find talking difficult, statues can be a way into working with a partner.

Clay moulding

Imagine your partner is a piece of clay and mould the clay into a statue.

Change roles.

Frozen together

One person makes a shape and freezes.

The partner finds a way of adding to the first person's shape to complete a statue and then freezes.

Statues from pictures

Take a magazine or postcard reproduction of a painting and, as a group, try to look like the picture.

Imagine the life of the people in the picture so you can show this before freezing.

Many of these ideas can be developed into improvisation or mood and feelings expressed in sounds or a single sentence.

Suggest ideas for improvisation using characters and themes already performed by the group.

COMMUNICATING IN PAIRS

Rearranging the person

One of you arranges yourself on a chair. Close your eyes. Remember how you are sitting.

Your partner rearranges your position on the chair by making three changes, e.g. moving your head slightly to one side.

With eyes still closed you describe how you are sitting after the changes.

Then open your eyes and look at your rearranged position.

This exercise requires trust and it is important to emphasise that changes in the sitting position should be done carefully and not be awkward or difficult and uncomfortable.

Face to face

Without speaking, one person tries to express a need to a partner.

The partner responds to what seems to be asked.

Back to back

Two people sit back to back and talk about a given subject but they must stay back to back and not look at each other.

Face to face talking gibberish

Partners sit facing each other and think of a problem then, using gibberish, try to explain the problem to each other.

Many people with emotional disturbance find all communication difficult and it may take several weeks before the group feels confident to try any verbal communication.

WORKING IN SMALL GROUPS

Sculpts

In groups of four make sculpts on the themes of searching, waiting and complaining.

Each person in the sculpts must be a distinct character.

For example, waiting at the doctor's surgery each person must be a separate character with a reason to be there.

Group animals

Group of three or four people.

Everybody draws an image of an animal, real or imaginary.

Everybody then re-creates the same animal using sounds and movement.

The 'animals' meet and find ways of interacting.

Then everybody writes the life story of the same animal, how it develops from babyhood, the sounds it makes, feeding habits, likes and dislikes, connections with other animals.

The group share the life story of each animal then create an environment where all the animals can live together.

All the animals then inhabit their environment.

These kinds of story have resonances for each person and connections with each person's life. In the safety of the drama room they can create metaphors and symbols which can make meanings and their own issues can be explored through the lives of the characters created in drama.

The leader can help to make this safe by facilitating the creating of the metaphors in a safe way through the structure and boundary of the drama.

WHOLE GROUP IDEAS

Creating an environment

Create an environment in the room using objects in the room.

When you are satisfied with what you have made, inhabit the space as a person in that place, using movement, mime and dialogue.

The place can be, for example,

a beach,

a park,

a supermarket,

a railway station.

The safe place

Find and inhabit the place in the room which is safest for you.

Inhabit the place making your body as comfortable as possible.

Then find the unsafest place in the room and inhabit that place in the most uncomfortable way you can.

Can you remember your safe place as a child?

Did you have a den? Was it under the table where you could play undisturbed or at the bottom of the garden?

Now make a 'den' together as a group, using objects in the room.

When it is complete, inhabit it as children would, making yourselves into the 'gang' whose safe place it is.

The gang meets together to tell stories of exploits at school and round about the district.

Tell your stories then go home to tea.

All this work needs to be structured for the group and characters created so self confidence is developed and some trust established between members of the group and the leader.

EXAMPLE OF A GROUP

DRAMA WITH SCHOOL PHOBICS

This group of children between the ages of eight and fourteen experienced severe difficulties in attending school and had prolonged absences from school because of this anxiety. They were not disaffected adolescents 'bunking off' from school.

The children exhibited such characteristics as:

anxiety and depression about school in general,

parents unable to get the child to school,

violent signs of fear of school when actually approaching the building,

severe emotional upset with temper tantrums,

unhappiness and a tendency to complain of symptoms without any objective signs, especially just before setting off for school,

anxiety about sharing the company of children of any age and an inability to mix with their peer group,

gross lack of self confidence,

no significant self-image,

anxiety about what was happening at home while they were away.

How the children played

The playing followed the same pattern for most of the children. An initial period of regressive play: being babyish, naughty, silly. There was little structure in this play but lots of fun for the children.

There followed a period playing robots, automata, zombies, clowns. Then a final stage of play which was much more complex. The children structured scenes from themes which were significant for them. Three important themes emerged: heroes who died, betrayals, homemaking and/or breaking.

Nobody played school.

Regressive play

For some children this was just a means of starting work in drama. A kind of warming-up process. For others the opportunity to express their ideas was so exciting that they couldn't control the process and over-reacted to the stimulus. For example, a play about eating their favourite cakes until they were sick went a little over the top. All the group rushing round the room, retching, being sick, flushing the lavatory in perfect mime until they all collapsed in laughter.

For these children it was a matter of learning about the process of putting feelings and ideas into dramatic form to make a statement about themselves. They were eager to learn but also liked permission to be silly sometimes.

However, another group of children simply played as much younger children, seeming to go through a process they had missed. They were quite serious and concentrated while playing. One boy went so far as to regress to babbling and baby talk for several sessions. He told me that given the chance he would do nothing but play for a whole year.

Stereotypes: robots, zombies, clowns

This emerged as a halfway stage towards making scenes and improvisations for themselves. The children wanted to be robots, clowns, mechanical dolls or, in the case of Jim, he died and rose from the dead as a zombie.

The play suggested by the children was for me to take the robots, dolls, etc., out of their boxes, wind them up or plug them in then set them tasks to perform. I had to suggest the tasks. Then things happened. Sometimes the dolls wound down or the robots lost their power, bits of them went rusty or fell off and I had to mend them. Sometimes their internal mechanisms went wrong and they refused to obey and did all kinds of forbidden things until they were put back in their boxes. These were powerful rituals and were constantly repeated throughout the course of our meetings.

With Jim and perhaps some of the others what we played as zombie and master was an exploration of the trust between adults and child, playing with this relationship until it was comfortable enough and safe enough to explore other feelings.

Structured scenes

This was the final phase of work where the groups explored many themes of betrayal, death and homemaking and breaking.

Heroes who died

This was enacted by two boys, John and Peter, aged 8 and 9. John thought up the story and throughout it was clearly 'his play'.

John said that it was winter and snowy weather and he was climbing a mountain on a rescue mission for farm animals and got stuck in the snow. Peter was an ambulance man who came to rescue him, got him down the mountain into the ambulance and hospital but on trying to revive John discovered he was dead.

This enactment was very dramatic, John crying for help, the ambulance's siren wailing, carrying John down the mountain and the final climax in hospital when after much hitting of John's heart he was pronounced 'dead'.

The boys acted this many times, often swapping roles. Then John asked if I could conduct a burial service after he had 'died'. So I gave a grand funeral oration about brave, good, kind John, greatly misunderstood when he was alive, but it was too late now ... John nodded approval from the grave.

The death *and* burial were very important for John. He had done his best, nobody cared, so he died to punish the world. This death scene continued for some weeks then John said he wanted to change the ending so that Peter's attempts at revival were successful and John didn't die but recovered. After the recovery both went to the palace to receive a bravery medal from the queen.

It is often difficult for the leader to stay with the children's stories if they include death but John was clear about the nature of his story and that it was a story.

It is interesting that the change to an optimistic ending coincided with John's successful return to school for two days a week.

Betrayal

This was a scene written and played by two 15 year old boys, Mark and Jason.

Mark was physically small and immature, Jason emotionally clinging, desperately seeking approval. Jason was full of imaginative ideas, Mark more practical but loved playing. Jason had the initial idea for the scene but both boys worked on it together and wrote a script of which they were very proud.

In the play, Mark was the pilot of a plane flying to America and Jason was his co-pilot but really a hijacker who had killed the co-pilot. The hijacker held up the plane and told the pilot to fly to Russia as he (the hijacker) had been a spy for the Russians for the past twenty years. The plane lands in Russia. The hijacker opens the plane door expecting a warm welcome but he is shot dead. The captain pushes his body out of the plane then flies back to Britain.

The climax was always played with great power. Jason opens the plane door expecting adulation, his expression changes to horror as he gets shot then a final rejection as he is pushed out of the plane to die in the place he thought was safe.

The character reversals were important. Jason changed from co-pilot to hijacker, Mark from kindly pilot to coolly indifferent person as he pushed Jason from the plane.

The story had great personal meaning for Jason and Mark.

For Jason, don't trust anyone, loyalty is not repaid; for Mark, be indifferent to other people, it's safer to be solitary. This was an expression of their life experience so far.

Homemaking and homebreaking

David and Paul were 12. Their play was devised together and they negotiated the theme and story between themselves. For two solitary boys this was important.

The play was set in the past, hundreds of years ago. Two young boys ran away from home because their parents were cruel to them. They set sail in a ship and roamed the world for many years. Then there was a great storm and they were shipwrecked and they landed on a desert island. The central theme of the scene was how the boys made a home on the island. David made the house and Paul caught the food while both of them had adventures being chased by giant crabs. In play David made his home very secure while Paul improvised the catching of fish for food. Then they made a scene where they went back to their shipwrecked boat and salvaged a knife, tins of rice pudding and even a rowing boat. Catching fish for food was becoming too difficult, a tin of rice pudding had greater appeal.

They both lived a comfortable orderly life on the island, until one day many years later Paul was poisoned by a fish which stung him while out fishing. He crawled up the beach to David but couldn't be saved by medicine, so died. This left David on his own for some years until he, too, died of a heart attack.

The important part of the scene for the boys were the tasks they had to do, making the house, keeping it clean, fishing. The relationship between the boys centred round these tasks. The boys said the scene was very important because it represented the kind of life they would like to have, making a safe home away from other people where they could be perfectly content.

Work with an individual child

Peter made his own play and refined the text and his performance over four weeks prior to his return to school. He began by saying he wanted to build a café. I was the builder's merchant and he phoned me for supplies, bricks, wood, slate for the roof. Then when the building was complete, I supplied furniture. Peter set out the tables and chairs, the cutlery and plates, etc., and waited for customers.

Then a family came into the café for a meal. They were very rude about the food in the café, sending things back until the owner threw them all out. We played this story a few times then Peter changed the story. When the family came into the café, each member asked for a particular dish of food and each time the waiter brought the wrong food. The family got angry and threw the food about. Then the waiter kicked them off the chairs and threw them out of the café.

He wrote the story with his teacher at school.

The Café

One day I phoned the builders. The table got stuck in the van. The builders tried to take the table out. They got the table out. They set the table out and the chairs and the café was ready.

The naughty family came in and sat down and the waiter said, 'What do you want?' 'I'll have fish and chips,' said the boy and the waiter brought meat balls and the boy kicked the plate off and the waiter threw him out on the road. Then the waiter said to Mr Smith, 'What do you want?' and Mr Smith said, 'I'll have a Sunday dinner,' and the waiter said, 'Yes, Mr Smith,' and brought him fish and chips. Mr Smith kicked the waiter up the backside. Then Mr Smith shouted at the waiter. Then a girl in the family, called Jane, shouted at the waiter. Then the waiter kicked them all out of his café onto the pavement and the naughty family didn't come back ever again.

In reality Peter was controlled by his father so enjoyed playing a bossy character. He learnt to be assertive in play which helped him make the return to school.

8

Drama with the abused person

There are a variety of ways of using the experience of drama to help children and adults who have been abused to build a more positive sense of self.

Abuse is usually defined as physical, emotional and sexual abuse. Many clients in groups will have experienced multiple abuse and virtually all abuse is an emotional abuse, disempowering the person and taking away self esteem. With all forms of abuse the survivors can be left with feelings of worthlessness, a sense that they are objects to be abused rather than people in their own right. Body boundaries have been so violated by aggression or through the emotional or sexual gratification of others that it becomes hard to value the self as a person with rights and needs.

THE ABUSE OF PEOPLE WITH DISABILITIES

Since this book was first written, new evidence has emerged which sadly suggests that people with disabilities are the group in society most likely to be subjected to some form of abuse.

D. Sobsey (1994) suggests that if definitions of abuse relate to severe forms of abuse and multiple victimisations of the same individuals, the relative risk for people with disabilities is probably at least twice as high and may be five or more times as high as for the general population.

People with disabilities are especially at risk from sexual abuse or assult. Senn (1988) suggested from a number of studies that 39%–68% of girls with developmental disabilities and 16%–20% of boys with developmental delay will be sexually abused before the age of 18.

The sexual abuse typically experienced by people with disabilities will be severe and chronic.

Perpetrators

The Abuse and Disability Project at the University of Alberta provided an analysis of 215 cases. The four most prevalent categories of offenders were disability service providers, acquaintances and neighbours, natural family members and peers with disabilities. (D. Sobsey (1994))

Almost half the offenders contacted their victims through special services provided because of the disability.

Power relationships

It is important to recognise that the abuse of people with disabilities will continue if our attitudes to disability reinforce inequality and if the rights of those with disabilities are disregarded or not prioritised.

It is important that those who offer care for people with disabilities do not abuse the relationship and do not try to develop an inappropriate dependency to meet their own needs.

Group leaders have a great responsibility to keep all members of the group safe from any form of abuse and that means constantly monitoring their own responses to their role so that the rights of the individuals in the group are respected and validated.

WHY DRAMA?

Drama is an appropriate way to help heal the hurts of abuse through finding ways to validate the person and explore roles and identities which lead towards self determination. There are many appropriate themes to help in the healing process. Ways of working and themes to be explored need to be negotiated with the group.

It is important to emphasise the health of the group or negotiate a particular task which will be of value. Many people who have experienced abuse survive through forms of defensive behaviour which have served them well. Sometimes these defence mechanisms can be counter-productive in different circumstances such as the group but if people feel supported and develop trust then individuals can find a place to relax and not need to be constantly watchful. This in itself can begin the healing process: finding the safe place with people who can be trusted.

It can be appropriate to use the strategies which helped in coping with abuse in the past (such as the capacity to distract, to withdraw into the imagination and be watchful of others) in more positive ways as part of drama learning. These mechanisms once used negatively can now be used to develop roles in drama, storymaking and storytelling and forms of dramatic improvisation.

DRAMA MODELS

The group may decide on task based work perhaps to help both children and adults reclaim their bodies after abuse or help children understand body boundaries and good and bad touching. Or Creative-Expressive drama work can establish high levels of self esteem in the group and self advocacy is a way to become a survivor.

TASK BASED GROUP FOR YOUNG CHILDREN WHO HAVE BEEN SEXUALLY ABUSED

The themes of such a group could be:

1 body awareness,

2 being assertive,

3 communication skills.

Body awareness

Body awareness play would be based on the movement work described in Chapter 5 to help children become aware of different parts of their bodies. Play can be based around activities such as rolling, rocking, stretching but must always reinforce the children's autonomy over their own bodies and develop an awareness of naming body parts and general body sensation. It is important for children who have been sexually abused to experience their bodies in other ways than sexual.

A gradual working towards what Sherbourne calls 'against' movements can help but the process must be carefully monitored so that the group are able to be successful.

Back to back

Pushing against another child in the group when two children sit back to back with their knees bent up.

Place your feet on the ground with a firm wide base in front and hands on the ground behind.

Then push backwards against each other to see how strong your partner is.

Engine

Partners sit back to back.

One of you is the 'engine' who pushes the other around the room, giving a ride over the floor.

For children who have been abused a back-to-back relationship can be safer than face to face and confidence can gradually be built up.

Games and songs about parts of the body can be incorporated into the sessions so children become familiar with naming the body and drawing and naming body parts.

It is important to reinforce respect for each other's body in the group and activities such as drawing round another's body is not appropriate for children who have been sexually abused.

Information about 'good' and 'bad' touching could be explored through scenes in drama or taught elsewhere, with the drama group being reserved for freer symbolic play about power relations and helping children develop assertion skills. Shared teaching could be helpful but the two leaders would have to exchange information about how children responded to information given and how they played in the drama group. That would be agreed as one of the boundaries of the group.

Learning about 'good' and 'bad' touching has to be reinforced with children showing general examples like pushing, pinching, hard tickling, before specific examples of sexually inappropriate touching. There are many illustrated books which can be used like *It's My Body* (1982), *My Book, My Body* (1989), and *A Very Touching Book* (1983). These are useful with younger children. *Look Back, Stride Forward* (1989) is an excellent book for older children and adolescents.

Assertion skills

Play in the drama group could be about assertion skills on a general level with simple scenes in pairs: one person trying to

persuade the other to do something the other doesn't want.
For example:

Selling

A shop assistant tries to sell a pair of shoes to a
customer and the customer doesn't want to buy.

Holding your own

A game for couples: each person decides on a topic to
talk about.

Partners sit close to each other and look at each other
throughout the game.

The two talk at once about their own topics.

Both continue talking until the leader tells them to
stop.

The aim is to keep talking at all costs and try to stop
the partner's concentration.

Suggestions of topics. Tell a fairy story. The way from
your house to school. Your most embarrassing
moment. Your last birthday party.

Fortunately/unfortunately

Partners

A and B

A starts telling a story beginning 'Fortunately'

B continues the story starting with 'Unfortunately'

Something like:

A   Fortunately, we were going on a picnic

B   Unfortunately, it began to rain

A   Fortunately, we had an umbrella

B   Unfortunately . . .

And so on.

Distraction game

Partners

One of you chooses a nursery rhyme, song or poem to
perform aloud.

Begin to speak/sing.

Your partner has to distract you by, for example, making funny faces, to make you stop talking and start laughing.

Picking a fight

A and B

A starts talking, 'No, you didn't'.

B continues, 'Yes I did'.

Go on talking making up a really strong argument.

Example	You are on the way to school and start the argument.
Suggestion	Use mime only, argue in a whisper, stand back to back.

Communication skills

The final theme of the programme would be to help children with communication skills and through that work give the message that it is not always possible to stop being hurt but that you can try to tell somebody. In this work it is important not to make the children feel they have failed if they can't be assertive and say, 'No,' because in reality children are small and their abusers large and powerful.

Communication games

What am I like?

Partners

Talk to your partner about yourself from the point of view of somebody else, such as your teacher or your sister.

Tell what you look like.

Your interests.

What you do at weekends and so on.

Remember from the point of view of somebody else.

Involvement without hands

Partners

Decide on an inanimate or animate object.

Set it in motion between you without using your hands but use the rest of your body.

Something like pushing a car that won't start or moving an elephant.

Gibberish selling

Partners

Try to demonstrate or sell something to your partner using only gibberish not language.

My story

Partners: A and B

A Tell me about the . . . elephant.

B Never mind that, tell me about . . .

Develop the dialogue

Partners: A and B

Choose one of the following dialogues and develop it into drama:

No. 1

A A man came to see me.

B Oh, when?

A While you were out.

B What did he want?

A He didn't say.

No. 2

A And that's what I told him.

B That was brave of you.

No. 3

A Well after that what more can I say?

B I can see it must have been difficult.

A Difficult!

Stories

For younger children there are many fairy stories about abused children which could be used as a starting point for play about communication: *Hansel and Gretel, Cinderella, Baba Yaga the Witch*, an African story called *The Orphan and the Tree*. All these stories show children coping with cruelty and explain some of the comfort the children received. Hansel and Gretel have each other; Cinderella has the Fairy Godmother; in *Baba Yaga*, Vasilissa, the heroine, has a doll which she feeds and is told what to do; the Orphan is nurtured by gifts from her dead mother, for water and fruit-bearing trees come forth from the place where the mother is buried.

Scenes from these stories can be used to encourage children to find a trusted adult to 'tell' if they are in trouble. For example, a scene from *Cinderella* where the Fairy Godmother is told by Cinderella how difficult it is to stay with her step-sisters and how unkind they are to her. Or Hansel and Gretel talking about their home as they get lost in the wood.

Perhaps bring the scenes into the present and ask what they could do now. So maybe Cinderella could phone 'Childline' and ask for help.

CREATIVE-EXPRESSIVE GROUP

Developing sensory awareness

If children are reasonably safe from abuse, some drama to develop sensory awareness can be a pleasure and fun for them. They have previously had to block out such sensation to spare themselves the pain of feeling the hurt of hitting or sexual abuse.

Sensory play with balloons and bubbles and a 'feeling box' full of objects with different textures and smells can create great excitement and pleasure for children frightened and frozen by abuse.

Balloons 1

Move around the room as if you are blown up like a balloon.

Move as if you are blown up to be a large balloon, then as if most of the air has been let out.

Make a group balloon with five people then see what happens when some of the air is let out, and when all of the air goes and the balloon collapses.

Balloons 2

Take a real balloon and blow it up.

Touch the balloon, tap it lightly in the air with the tips of your fingers.

Gently touch the balloon and stroke it.

Get into groups of four and play with the balloons together.

Tie the balloons together with string then continue until all the balloons in the group are tied together.

Draw a picture of your balloon and imagine how it felt being part of the big group.

Using smells

Bring a smell to the group.

Work with a partner.

Smell the smell and talk about what the smell makes you feel.

Make up a story which incorporates the smell in some way.

The Smelly Monster

The whole group make a monster together which spits out the worst smell in the whole world and frightens off everybody because of the smell.

Storymaking for adults and children

There are many children's books which describe children's less than perfect relationships with their families. They can be used in drama by groups of children who are the survivors of abuse but also by adults to help get in touch with their childhood relationship with parents.

Picture books create very powerful images which can stimulate drama work.

Not Now, Bernard

One such book is *Not Now, Bernard* by David McKee (1980) which tells the story of a small boy called Bernard who cannot attract the attention of his parents who are busy with household tasks. Even when Bernard goes into the garden and is eaten by a monster and the monster returns and takes Bernard's place his parents still ignore the Monster/Bernard. The book ends with the Monster in bed, saying:

'But I'm a monster,' said the monster.
'Not now, Bernard,' said Bernard's mother.

This book expresses the sense of helplessness the child feels in the face of parental indifference, still getting no attention when turning into a monster. The parents are legitimately busy with washing up and other parental tasks but this is no help to the child.

The resonances are strong and the dramatisation of this simple story can be powerful.

It is easy for the whole group to act the story in groups of three, two parents and the child Bernard/Monster. It works effectively if enacted as the leader narrates the story. In most groups the 'actors' quickly pick up the dialogue of the story and can join in the narration.

At the end of the enactments the participants are asked to stay in their threes but to make an inner circle with the parents and an outer circle with Bernard, the two groups facing each other and communicating with the Bernards in the outer circle and the parents in the inner circle facing Bernard. I ask the Bernards to keep repeating the line,

But I'm a monster.

and the parents,

Not now, Bernard.

shouting as loud as possible to experience shouting but no communicating. The leader stops the shouting after three or four repetitions.

It can be a very freeing activity to be able to shout your complaint as Bernard but also to experience the frustration of not being heard by the adults. Playing the parents can cause ambivalence about loving, yet feeling guilty and irritated by the child.

This story although written for children is a powerful piece for adults and enables them to get in touch with their feelings as a child. The power of the story and the feelings it brings up for adults often surprise the group and the sadness it some-times engenders should be worked with by the leader.

Strange Animal

This is an African story and clearly describes power relations in families. It is a story for children of nine years and upwards and is also very effective with adults.

There was once a boy who lived in Africa and in his family everybody was always telling him what to do: his grandparents, mother and father, older brothers and most of all his aunt. Now she was the worst, always telling him to go here and there, do this and that. Not only that, but she shouted her orders in such a loud voice that the birds screeched back from the trees.

The boy didn't like his aunt and wanted to get some bad medicine to put in her food to make her less noisy but he never did. He only thought about it and he always obeyed his aunt. His father said that he must obey and do what his aunt told him to do.

The boy thought about being grown up and being able to shout back at his aunt. He dreamed about that time.

The boy's aunt knew of a place where lots of fruit grew and she wanted the boy to go there. It was quite far away, a scary place with caves and strange places. The boy's friend had told him about a strange animal which lived in one of the caves and frightened those who went to pick fruit.

But the aunt said that the boy must go and pick fruit, so he went although he was afraid. He began to pick the fruit from the trees but after a while he heard a rustle in the bush beside him. He stopped picking and stood still. Out of the bush came the strange animal just as his friend described and the boy stood still, very frightened. He quickly took out his little drum which he always carried with him and began to beat it. The strange animal stopped, looked at the boy and began to dance.

The boy played the drum all day and the animal danced and the boy knew that while the animal danced it could not harm him. As the sun went down and night came the animal grew tired, stopped dancing and ran into the bush back to its cave.

The boy walked home but his aunt was waiting, still shouting, wanting her fruit. As there was no fruit she began to beat the boy until he escaped and hid in his own hut.

The next day the boy told his father what had happened

and his father believed him. His aunt did not believe him and said he had lied about the strange animal. She began to shout again.

The boy's father said that they should all go to the place tomorrow. The aunt thought that this was silly but if she went she could shout at the boy all day, so she came. When the family arrived at the place and the tree with the fruit there was no strange animal. They began to pick fruit and the aunt called the boy to give her his drum which she hung on a high branch of a tree where it was difficult for the boy to reach. She told the boy to pick fruit and not be so idle.

The boy obeyed but he also listened for the strange animal which he knew would appear sooner or later. When the strange animal came, it immediately ate the boy's father and mother. The aunt tried to run away but the animal caught her and ate her, too.

The boy reached up to the branch of the tree and finally grabbed hold of his drum and began to play.

The boy played faster and faster and the animal danced faster and faster until finally out of his mouth flew the boy's father and mother.

Then the boy began to play slower and slower. The boy's father told him to play faster and faster so the animal would spit out the aunt.

'Must I?' said the boy.

'Yes, you must', said his father.

So the boy beat his drum, reluctantly at first but soon he beat faster and faster until the aunt was spat out of the animal's mouth.

It became dark and the animal went back to its cave and the family began the journey home.

The aunt was very quiet all the way back and after that day she never shouted at the boy again. Being swallowed by a strange animal had shocked the aunt who decided it was a waste of time to shout. So much better just to sit in the sun,

And the boy was happy with this.

Working with the story
Before telling the story the group can warm up with another game.

Master/Servant game

Partners

One chooses to be Master, the other Servant.

The Master has to give tasks to the Servant who carries them out until she doesn't want to do something then she says, 'No'.

As soon as the Servant says, 'No,' and refuses to carry out a task, you become the Master and the Master becomes the Servant.

You keep the roles until the Servant again refuses a task and says, 'No,' and so becomes Master.

The tasks can be jobs such as carrying a chair across the room, bowing three times or any mindless activity the Master chooses.

The Master should be bossy.

After playing the game the leader starts to tell the story, and tells it up to the line

'His father said he must obey his aunt and do what she told him to do.'

Boy/Aunt game

Ask the same partners as in the Master/Servant game to choose the roles of aunt and boy but this time not to change roles. The aunt must give the boy tasks to do, shouting at him all the time, and the boy must obey.

This continues until the leader gives the signal to stop.

The leader continues the story up to the line,

'The boy's friend had told him about a strange animal . . .'

Then ask the whole group as individuals to imagine they are the boy and to draw the place with the caves where the fruit grew and, on the other side of the paper, the strange animal as they imagine it.

After they have done the drawings, they share these images in small groups of three or four.

The leader continues with the story until the line,

'stopped dancing and ran into the bush, back to its own cave.'

Then ask the group to get into the aunt and boy pairs. The

boy stays the boy and the aunt becomes the strange animal. The boy improvises a drum and beats the drum and the strange animal starts to dance. The boy can experiment with stopping the drum to see what the strange animal does. Then he continues beating the drum faster and faster until the animal gets tired and as night falls the animal stops dancing and runs through the bush back to its cave.

The leader continues reading the story until the line,

'And hid in his own hut.'

And then asks the group as individuals still to imagine they are the boy and to write a letter to the father.

The leader continues the story until the end of the family's adventure with the animal before they make their journey home. The group re-enacts the scene where the aunt is inside the animal.

The leader chooses someone to be the boy, the father and the aunt. The rest of the group can be the strange animal surrounding the aunt who has been swallowed. The leader asks the aunt to plead for her life with the boy, shouting from inside the monster; the father instructs the boy to play the drum and in his own time the boy must obey and the aunt is thrown out of the monster's mouth.

When this scene is over, the leader tells the story to the end.

The pairs who were aunt and boy take those roles and talk together about what has happened and what their relationship will be like in the future.

After five minutes, stop.

Everybody in the group sits in a circle and acts as the boy in the story.

The leader goes round the group and asks everyone to speak for one minute at the most on the thoughts of the boy in the story.

The group can share many ideas about being a child and being an adult in the family and the use and misuse of power which are all relevant themes for drama with abused people. The exploration of these issues is well distanced through the story so the group can explore the themes in safety through the characters of the story.

In this way storytelling can be part of a healing process where relationships can be explored symbolically through the form of a story.

Themes about monsters

One of the recurring themes which is important for those who have been abused is about dealing with monsters. In stories and tales about monsters of every kind, there are many strategies, from confronting the monster, to tricking the monster, to enduring the monster until better times come around.

All these themes can be explored through stories and visual images and it is important for the leader and the group to find stories and images which have particular resonances for them.

STORIES

For children stories about strategies for dealing with monsters can be part of a healing process that gives them a chance to play the monster in drama and also to trick the monster or challenge monstrous behaviour.

Animal stories are enjoyed by children. This one describes ways of coping with and tricking the monster lion.

Hello, House

Lion was walking in the forest under a tree where the bees had a nest. The bees were busy near their nest and one bee landed on Lion's nose. He was so scared that he stung the lion.

Lion was very angry and screeched and roared in his pain. 'You stupid bees, I'll set fire to your nest and burn you all.'

The bees pleaded with Lion, said they were very sorry and gave him a honeycomb.

Lion was pleased with his present and said he would collect it later on his way home from his walk through the jungle. He went on his way.

Lion hadn't been gone very long when Mr and Mrs Hare came by. 'Look at that honeycomb!' said the Hare. 'Let's eat it for breakfast!'

So Mr and Mrs Hare sat down and ate the honeycomb and skipped off into the jungle.

Back came Lion. He gave a great roar and said, 'Where is my honeycomb?'

The bees told Lion that Mr and Mrs Hare had been by and eaten up his honeycomb.

'Oh, ho,' said the Lion, 'That's the last meal they will eat. Tell me where they live and I'll go and kill them!' The bees said they didn't know where the Hares lived and Lion went roaring away.

He asked everybody he met but nobody wanted to tell him because he frightened everybody. At last poor little Master Weasel told Lion that they lived over the top of the hill.

Then Master Weasel ran off as fast as he could to warn the Hares that the Lion was coming to kill them.

Mr and Mrs Hare ran out of their house and hid under some bushes some way along the track.

By and by Lion came along the track. Mr Hare followed Lion's footprints and saw they stopped outside Hare's house. 'Ah,' thought Hare, 'I bet Lion is in my house waiting to eat me up.' Hare went to stand some way from the house and called out, 'Hello, House, Hello, House.'

No answer.

Lion was hidden in the house behind the closed door waiting for the Hares to come home so he could eat them up. Lion licked his lips thinking he would soon be eating hare.

Hare called again and there was no answer.

Hare said, 'This is strange. Every day when I come home I say "Hello, House", and if there is nobody at home the House replies, "Hello, Hare". Today there was no reply from the house. I think there must be someone there.'

Lion heard from inside the house and thought, 'I'd better answer.'

'Perhaps my house is deaf,' said Hare, 'I'll shout louder.' So at the top of his voice Hare cried, 'Hello, House.'

And the Lion shouted back, 'Hello, Hare.'

'Ah, Lion,' cried Hare, 'Are you there waiting to eat me? Whenever did you hear of a house talking?' Hare ran off and hid in the bushes.

Lion came out of the house. He felt such a fool. He searched for Hare but couldn't find him. Then he got tired and went home. He told everyone he met that Hare was such a miserable creature.

'Eat him? Not I. The thought of it makes me feel sick!'

This story has many dramatic moments when Lion is

monstrous and when he is tricked in a variety of ways. There are also moments when Lion is too frightening and he gets what he wants which is the experience of children who are abused. So at many moments the story has resonances but in the end Lion is tricked and his power diminished by his stupidity.

These kinds of story can be used to great effect with children who are trying to come to terms with the monsters in their own lives and in play for a moment they can sting Lion on his nose. What pleasure!

Communicating about sex

It is very important that people who have been abused can put their experiences into a framework of sexual information.

This information may be given to the group elsewhere but it can be helpful, particularly if members of the group have learning disabilities, to explore aspects of this information through communication and drama games. This will help individuals in the group to explore their attitudes and feelings about sexual matters.

Babette Cole's book *Mummy Laid an Egg* (1993) has the children giving a talk to the parents about how babies are born after the parents tell the children a

'load of rubbish'

about the facts of life.

The parents try to avoid telling the children about the facts of life. This could easily be dramatised with members of the group playing the embarrassed parents and the clued-up children giving the lecture to the parents.

This is a reversal of the usual power dynamic in families but may not be appropriate if a parent has in reality been unable to protect the child from abuse or has been a perpetrator.

In *Let's Talk About Sex* (1994) by R.H. Harris, there is a great deal of clear information about growing up and sexual matters. The book is very well illustrated and there are two characters, the bird and the bee, who make amusing comments on the information in the book. The bee finds the information very embarrassing at times.

These two characters could be played by members of a group as they respond to the information in the book and explore how they feel about it.

For example, at the beginning of the book the two have a conversation about reading the book:

Bee   Oh . . . my goodness! This is a book on . . .

Bird Sex. Do you have a problem with that?

Bee   I certainly do! I'll stick to the stars thank you.

Sometimes when exploring the issues which emerge as part of the aftermath of abuses it is helpful to explore through symbolic forms, as this acts as a container for raw and difficult feelings.

Many survivors have very negative feelings about themselves and their sexuality and aspects of this self loathing can be explored in symbolic form. I often use children's picture books for this purpose.

For example, *Prowlpuss* (1994) by G. Wilson is a beautifully illustrated book about a rather randy alley-cat who goes out to visit his lady-love. She ignores him so he goes back home to old Nelly Smith who cares for him.

Prowlpuss has many of the characteristics of an unattached abused person expressing a yearning for an idealised love. A group could explore the images of the randy tough-as-boots cat, the idealised beautiful love object of his desire and the down-to-earth old lady who welcomes old Prowlpuss back from his wanderings.

These roles could be expanded, developed, changed as the group improvise.

ADULT GROUPS

Themes

Adult groups often want to explore the same themes as children. One of the more powerful images for adults is about the 'monsters' ever present in our lives, be it time, money, people. Images and stories abound.

I often use visual images to introduce this theme. There are, for example, two sets of postcards from the National Gallery called Beasts and Angels and some of the illustrations could be used with some groups. Others may find the beasts too gruesome or too sexual.

Picasso has many illustrations of monsters, in particular images of the Minotaur, that mythical creature half man, half bull. I use some of these images as stimulus material to begin to focus on the theme. For Picasso, the Minotaur was a constant image. He said (1987),

'If one were to trace a line linking all of the places where I've lived in my life, one might end up with a drawing of a Minotaur.'

It can be as important for adults who have been abused as for children to begin to explore their abuse and oppression in symbolic form, making images and metaphors through the medium of drama.

This is one way I work with the theme of Monsters.

Monsters

Warm-up

Play Master/Servant. (See the story 'Strange Animal' p. 133)

Show illustrations of 'monsters'. General discussion.

Monsters have power. They oppress.

What is monstrous in your life at the moment?

Development

Individual monsters

In small groups people individually draw images to represent what are the particular monsters in their lives at the moment of drawing: be it too little time to get everything done or the boss at work.

Choose themes that can be safely explored in the group.

The small group share each monster.

Group monsters

With objects and material in the room small groups create a monster which incorporates the main theme of each individual in the group.

Showing the monster

The small-group monster is then presented to the larger group.

Coping with the monster

Small-group members then discuss between themselves how to deal with their group monster.

What strategies will you use?

Confront it and destroy it. If so, how?

Trick it in some way? What tricks will you use?

Or endure the monster? What does that do to you?

Or a combination of strategies.

Make a sculpt or an enactment of your strategy.

Show to the rest of the group.

This theme structured in this way can be exhilarating and produce powerful drama. It can be a beginning, a way forward and a release through acknowledging a shared experience.

STORIES BY ABUSED CHILDREN

As part of the healing process in drama, I work with individual children using play and drama as a means of healing the hurts of abuse. Many children write stories for themselves. This is a story by an 8 year old girl who created an island out of clay and Playdoh. The island was green and the sea surrounding it was purple. This is the story:

Anna's Island

There was once an island called Anna's Island in a magic country and this island was surrounded by purple sea. On the island were four monsters and they lived on the rocky part of the island. They lived together and they fought. The bit of the island they lived on was once nice but they had made it horrible.

There was stranded seaweed on this part of the island and the monsters ate the seaweed. They also ate people and Anna's family as well.

Anna was alone on the island except for her dog. There were bones and skeletons of the people the monsters had eaten in little pieces and they mouldered on the island and all that part of the island stank with the monsters' smell.

The monsters had a 'fridge hidden in a secret place. Anna didn't know where it was but the monsters kept all the dead bodies there.

The sea outside of the island is rough. No animals live in it because they are too scared that the monsters will eat them. The leader of the monsters is called Terrible X. The rest of the island is calm but Anna has to stay awake all night in case the monsters come and spoil her part of the island.

Sometimes the dog is naughty and eats a piece of the bodies. Then Anna gets really mad but she doesn't smack the dog. The dog went to the bad part of the island and took a piece of the body. The dog talks and he lied to Anna about the meat.

Anna made a fire and found some food. It was magic oranges and she stored them away from the dog. If the monsters ate this food they would vanish so Anna put a big lump of it down for the monsters but there was a magic force which stopped the monsters eating the food.

Anna tried to make the food look like bodies but Trouble, the dog, found the food, sniffed it then told the other monsters that it didn't smell like bodies so they didn't eat it.

The master of the monsters was angry about the trick and his voice went booming over the island. Anna was afraid that the monsters would break the force field which was made of sand. Then they would be able to cross the island but the force field held and they couldn't pass.

So long as the barrier remains the island is safe for Anna. She has made herself a swimming pool and this is the safest place but at present she hasn't got any water left because the dog keeps drinking it.

THIS IS ANNA'S ISLAND, IT IS THE STORY SO FAR.

The monsters in Anna's life still haunt and the effort to keep them at bay requires twenty-four hour vigilance but Anna has found a metaphor for herself and she can explore her situation. A small help.

And this is John's island, his way of exploring his life as he begins to integrate his experiences.

He made his islands with 'slime' and used small dolls to inhabit them.

The Islands of Past, Present and Future

These islands exist in the sea of magic. The past island is blue, translucent, smooth, sticky, stretchy, cold, broken.
It is the longest island.

The present island is blue, muddy with an eye in the middle, a good eye sometime, sometime an evil eye.

The future island is green, the biggest island with a huge football in the middle which is egg shaped.
It is slimy, lumpy and bubbly. The football is safe from the lumpy edges.

On the island of the past lives a cowboy and Frankenstein.
They look after each other, sometimes they argue.
They are exploring together because they are friends and they found the island together. They found another two islands, but they left them.
They enjoy living on Past Island.

On the present island lives the Green Power Ranger.
He lives alone.
He misses his companions.
He was naughty being a Power Ranger so they sent him away and he found this place.
He just looks after it, makes sure no one comes because he wants it himself.

The future island is inhabited by a dragon.
He shares his space with a turtle and a tiger.
On the back of the dragon is a man that told the dragon to find the island and he flew around it until he found it then he brought his friends.
The man on the dragon's back is a warrior.

One day the islands come together and make one island and in the end they all learnt to live together and they don't argue so much and accept each other, the past, present and future.

9

Drama with multiply-disabled people

ESTABLISHING THE GROUP

It can be very daunting to try to establish a drama group for children or adults who are profoundly disabled. This group of people, who need the help of others to function, who initially appear so helpless, whose physical care takes up so much time and energy, can paralyse a leader before the group even begin. It is a powerful dynamic to establish communication and respect the individuality of people who are multiply disabled.

The adults who care for the profoundly disabled also experience frustration, despair, anger and hopelessness and so the leader of the drama group needs to acknowledge both the helplessness of the disabled and the stress of the carers. This can be very hard. Hopelessness can set in and creative ideas fly out of the window. Then it is difficult to devise a way of working with such a group. The leader and helpers for the group feel unable to think of ways to stimulate creativity. What can we possibly do with a person so dependent on others for care? Does this person have the capacity to engage in creative work? And the most basic question of all – what can we do to stimulate such a person?

Functioning of the group
Firstly it is essential to organise the functioning of the group. This means,

a helper for each group member,

clear arrangements for getting the group together,

who brings them and takes them back,

145

practical arrangements about the physical care for each person and,

emergency procedures for any problems which may arise.

CREATIVE-EXPRESSIVE GROUP

The aims would be:

1 to stimulate some communication and response from the group as appropriate to their level of functioning;

2 to establish relationships in the group as far as possible;

3 to establish trust and genuineness between group members and helpers by the acceptance of the individuality of each person in the group;

4 to offer creative experiences and sensory experiences which stimulate the group and go some way to meet their emotional needs.

ESTABLISHING COMMUNICATION IN ORDER TO BUILD RELATIONSHIPS

This is the primary task at the beginning of the group. Before communication can develop there must be observation of each individual in the group and explorations to find the most effective way to make the relationship. It is important to have an open mind about the capacities of each person because the freedom of the group can create a confidence which may not be there in other situations, so keep an open mind. This can be hard especially for helpers who may know the members well and can feel rejected by a person who makes a livelier response to the group than is experienced in the day-to-day care.

Relaxation

Make sitting on the floor the base of all this work.

This is the safest place from which to explore the environment.

Each member works with a helper.

Use gentle music to establish rocking movements, each member of the group holding hands with a partner/helper.

Use hands and arms in wave movements up and down the sides of the body facing your partner.

Move heads from side to side.

Curl up with arms round the knees then slowly open the body out and stretch.

Snail

Curl up like a snail, then let your partner/helper gently tickle your face or sing to you to persuade you to uncurl.

Chair

Helper cradles partner by sitting behind making her body into a 'chair' and rocks her partner gently from side to side, humming or singing to create vocal communication.

Body work

It is important to work on a developmental continuum with work which explores the participant as passive recipient, then as equal partner then as initiator of movement activities. This can all happen in one drama session if the participant can experience the body in each mode or it may be that the group need to move from passive to active participants in the course of the sessions.

Passive recipient

At the beginning of the session use the floor as the safe place and the helper as the person who will provide the physical security for the participant by supporting and containing her body and exploring different ways to do this. It is most important to offer these experiences in a way which does not overwhelm the participant.

The helper cradles her partner and rocks from side to side.

The helper lies down on her back, knees bent up, and her partner sits astride her knees so they face one another. The adult gently bounces her partner.

The helper lies full length on her stomach and her partner sits astride her back.

Equal partners

This is the stage when the participant begins to respond actively to movement play and may begin to initiate activities.

Lean against the helper from a sitting behind position, gently move from side to side.

Facing partner see-saw holding hands and leaning backwards and forwards. Make eye-contact and sing or hum while see-sawing backwards and forwards.

Initiator

This is the stage when the participant responds to her partner by actively moving her as part of the play.

Partner rolls the helper across the room. If rolling not possible partner pushes the helper's shoulders so the body moves a little.

Moving through the room

Explore the room by moving across the space in the easiest way.

Children who find difficulty moving could roll or crawl with their helpers supporting them. If this is not possible the helpers can carry or push them around the room so they can explore the space together and experience their bodies in the space of the room.

Creep across the room as quietly as possible.

Then (for those who can walk), stamp on the floor very fast, then very softly and slowly. Make sounds to accompany the movement.

Slide over the floor pulled along by the helper. Use a sheet of plastic if the room has a carpet or a sheepskin rug if the floor is wood or vinyl to make the sliding easier.

Move across the room, stop in the middle for a given moment then continue to the other side.

Move across the room, stop in the middle, make a sound or bang the drum then continue across the room.

Continue changing the activity in the middle of the room.

Tangling

Tangle everybody in the room in as complicated a shape as possible and try to move about the space.

When very tangled try to untangle.

(Those who can't move can be held or supported by their helper).

Sensory stimulation

Sensory environments

Make a sensory environment in the room to stimulate or relax the group. Use play equipment, tunnels, curtains and blocks to change the space into an environment which can be explored.

Tunnels to crawl through, blocks to climb, mats to roll over. Create a space where each person can explore at least some part of the room in a new way, crawling, climbing, rolling or being carried around.

Multiple sensation

Use sounds, light, water and music to change the room. Use a spotlight with a revolving colour wheel to change the light and colour in the room. Let the group simply experience the light and colour, relaxing as they see fit.

Use cushions or soft blocks or shapes to make different surfaces and heights in the room. Experience these changes by climbing or sitting in the new spaces.

Light and water

Light playing on water is a soothing experience if you have a water source, a spotlight and a revolving wheel to attach to the light. This can at times become too absorbing but is worth a try.

Run hands through water, then change the colour of the water or change the texture with soap or perfume to make the water softer.

Music can be used in all these exercises to stimulate relaxation or excitement according to the environments created.

Touch and taste and sight and smell

Use large amounts of jelly piled on a table with everything carefully protected so the group may touch and make a mess. This is an experience of touch, smell and taste which can be safely enjoyed. It can be particularly rewarding for those who have experienced being fed by a carer; just to be messy with food can be a freedom and a joy. Be warned, prepare the space carefully for all will be splattered. Use different coloured jelly for visual stimulation.

Treasure basket

Devise a treasure basket or bag full of objects to stimulate touch and other senses. A basket can be used for those who need to see all the items but some groups like to dip into a bag and pull out different items. The dynamic is very different according to whether objects are in a basket where they can be seen or a bag where the object is felt before being seen.

It is important to let the person examine all the objects and explore undisturbed unless they want to share the experience. The role of the helper is more to observe and be a supportive person, not necessarily to share the experience directly. Objects to look for: natural objects are best, for while plastic can be brightly coloured, the material itself is often uninteresting compared to natural objects made of wood, for example.

Elinor Goldschmied developed this idea with young children as a way to stimulate their senses. She suggests such objects as:

Metal objects

spoons, bunch of keys, small tins, small ash tray, tin trumpet, small funnel, small harmonica, a metal whistle, key rings linked together, small metal-framed mirror, bunch of bells, tins containing rice, dried peas, etc., tea strainer, bicycle bell.

Objects in leather, textiles, etc.

leather purse, high bouncer ball, velvet powder puff, small rag doll, leather spectacle case, small teddy bear, bunch of coloured ribbons, bath plug, bean bag, small cloth bags containing pot-pourri or lavender, thyme, etc., large rubber (eraser), tennis ball.

Paper, cardboard, etc.

greaseproof paper, rice paper, small cardboard boxes, cardboard tubes from lavatory rolls, little notebook, tinfoil, corrugated paper.

Children enjoy the exploration of such baskets and their attention will stay quite concentrated.

Choose objects which are safe for the group. Clearly the issue of safety comes first and for those with limited control of movement, objects which can injure would be excluded.

It is important to help the group experience what they want from the objects so the role of the helper will be to observe sympathetically and maintain the safety of the individual in her care. It is not necessary for her to interact with the individual child but to nurture from afar. Too often we impose too much of ourselves on those with profound disability and find it difficult just to let them be.

Using smells

Each helper brings a smell. It must be isolated so the smells don't get mixed up together.

Child and helper sniff the smell together and decide if it is a good smell or not.

They make sounds together which describe the smell.

Texture

Each helper brings in three items with different textures and puts them in separate bags.

All the bags go into the middle of the room and pairs (child and helper) choose a bag each.

They both feel inside the bag without looking at the contents.

They share words or sounds about the feelings evoked by touching the object.

They don't look at the contents of the bag until the memory of the texture is fading.

They choose another bag and repeat the experience.

Paper

Collect a pile of newspapers and the group can tear them into small pieces to create a snowstorm.

Make hats or objects for each other.

Use paper to become a creature and crawl around the room in your paper skin.

Crush paper into large balls and throw them around the room.

Balloons

Use thicker more durable balloons.

Blow them up and in pairs explore the balloon through touch.

Flick the balloons and watch them float around the room.

Move around the room with the balloon, holding it or tapping it or rolling with it or chasing it.

MAKING RELATIONSHIPS THROUGH SOUND AND VOICE

Sensitivity in the interaction

This is a most important aspect of drama with profoundly handicapped people which often needs ingenuity and persistence on the part of helpers and group leader. Finding a way to share aspects of yourself without disempowering the other can be complex. Sharing through holding, rocking and touching can be a way to establish communication but if not done with sensitivity and awareness of the needs of the disabled person it can also be an abuse reinforcing their sense of helplessness and disownership of their bodies. If helpers use holding and rocking members of the group as a way to establish a relationship there should also be activities which are shared or initiated by the participants. It is very important for those who experience physical intrusion of their bodily function every day because of their disability that their body is respected as belonging to them and that in play and drama, they have choices about sharing themselves with others. This can be communicated non-verbally by the care the leader and helpers take when instigating play.

Communicating with sounds and singing

The child begins by blowing, starting gently then getting noisier.

Working with a child the helper listens and follows the sounds being made.

When a sound is made, the helper imitates it.

The two make patterns with the sounds. The helper can begin.

Then add simple consonant sounds like b-b-b or d-d-d or m-m-m to make an interesting pattern of sound.

If the child cannot imitate the pattern, then she can begin with sounds and the helper elaborates and ends the sequence.

This kind of playing with sounds can develop a very strong communication between two people and can stimulate laughter and great sensory pleasure.

For those who can move, try feet on floor, hands clap, hands on knees, floor, etc.

For those who can't move, try finger clicks or claps.

Try human sounds like coughing, sneezing, laughing, singing, whistling.

Use percussion instruments, drums, woodblocks and sticks, xylophones, cymbals, etc.

Experience the sounds they make and try different rhythms, soft and loud.

Hum and sing to the music.

Try any of these activities, the helper moving close to the child then across the space in the room.

Leader tells a story and incorporates sounds made by the group into the story.

TELLING STORIES

Telling stories is a way to establish communication; even if the receiver of the story can't understand, the tone of voice and the vitality of the speaker/reader establishes a rapport.

Choose stories with repetition and rhythmic sections. Choose simple picture books with strong colours: books like *The*

Yellow Button (1990) which is beautifully illustrated, *Bye Bye Baby* (1989) for repetition and a wonderful story, and *The Bad Babies' Book of Colour* (1986) and *Titch* (1971) which have bright drawings.

DESCRIPTION OF A GROUP

I once worked with a group of three children, each with a student helper. The group met over a term of ten weeks. The children lived in an institution with school and hospital care available on site.

The three children were Jane, John and Peter. They were between the ages of 5 and 7. Jane was hyperactive, had behavioural difficulties, communication disorders, lack of co-ordination of muscular activity and partial sight. John was brain-damaged, with spastic lower limbs, physical handicaps and a communication disorder. Peter was brain-damaged, quadriplegic, epileptic with a physical handicap and a communication disorder. Jane moved freely, obsessively pacing round the room. John moved stiffly at times and Peter could not stand but could roll over on the floor. None of the children had language but all could make sounds of various sorts to communicate meaning.

The goals in working with the children were to develop certain motor skills, establish social contact with each other and the helpers and stimulate the use of sounds and movement and generally have fun.

The first session with the three children was an exploratory session for us all. It was a case of mutual observation of behaviour and discovering the boundaries. The children coped better than the rest of us. We tried too hard, forcing the pace, the children tested us out and we felt helpless wondering how best to 'give' and 'get something back'. At the end of the session our immediate reaction was relief that it was over, but when we thought in detail about what had happened and wrote down what we had observed we discovered that the children had responded in quite remarkable ways. This gave us confidence to develop the work with the children following their lead and using their responses to us.

It was after this first session that I and the students felt at our most helpless, we needed to talk together and write our observations and it was only at that point that we began to understand the importance of the small responses and communications that had been offered to us by the children and at that point our confidence returned. I wrote,

'Peter very responsive facially, smiles and laughs when you talk to him. Likes to look at himself in the mirror. Likes to be rocked and sung to. Can bang the drum. Can roll over twice if encouraged and widely applauded.

Jane rushed round the room, flung the curtains open, closed curtains, opened them. She likes the contrast between dark and light. Refused to make eye contact, then leapt on me and one of the helpers clinging to us sucking at our clothes. Likes the musical instruments. Listened to the sounds then off on her race round the room. Enjoys swinging in the air. Asked to be swung and responded to the freedom of the movement, then off on her circuit of the room again.

John amiable, likes the ground, listened to the music, likes listening to voices and singing but moving about causes alarm. Smiles as an instinctive response with little discrimination.'

The second week was more settled. We were accepted. We began to establish rituals for the group to develop a structure and trust between us. We began by rocking the children on our laps, we greeted each other, we sang our greetings, we attached ourselves to each other through making a spider's web by throwing a ball of wool to each other. We broke the wool, the attachment, and worked in pairs enjoying special rituals not common to the group. Jane always liked a swing, Peter liked his back patted while he sang and hummed, John liked to sing to the xylophone.

The children always led, we followed and tried to use their stimulus to achieve our goals. Jane's swinging encouraged Peter to roll over more than once and Peter's roll encouraged a dance from John.

Each week we followed old rituals and tried to expand the relationships. We always worked from the floor and returned to the safety of the floor after each activity. This was security for John and Peter but sometimes hard for Jane who liked to roam, but after intense physical activity she would let herself relax enough to accept us and even to make eye contact. At the end of the term we felt a regard for three people who had each a distinctive personality and temperament. We could see developments both social and physical in the whole group, the three participants, the helpers and leader.

SAND TRAY PLAY WITH AUTISTIC PEOPLE

One of the interesting findings in the study of autism as described in *Autism Explaining the Enigma* by U. Firth (1989) is the results of Block Design tests which show the skill of autistic children.

These tests involve the copying with little cubes of an abstract pattern, within a time limit. As a rule autistic children, provided that they can understand what is required, obtain scores as good as or better than those of normal children of the same age. It would seem that skill in these tests requires isolation of stimuli, favouring detachment, which is part of the pattern of abilities in autistic children who have low results on tests which require connection of stimuli favouring coherence.

This skill in visual patterning can be supported as a way to develop self esteem by the use of play with objects in a sand tray.

Blue cat-litter trays are appropriate containers for the sand; the blue of the tray can act as an image of water if required.

Small toys and other objects which can be placed in the sand can be collected by the group leader or people in the group.

Small family figures, farm animals, wild animals, soldiers, mythical creatures, characters from fiction, current favourites from TV, can all be used in play.

The sand is placed in the tray and a landscape created in the sand. Sometimes children like to make patterns in the sand without the figures, and this is very satisfying play.

When a landscape is created, figures are placed in the sand as and where the participant chooses to place them. This makes a landscape or a world for the figures placed in the sand.

Unlike normal children who would describe a context for the figures and perhaps narrate a story of the world they have created in the sand, autistic children usually describe the spatial connections between the objects without any context or story.

However, one of the interesting processes of communication can be the children describing the spatial configuration and the leader making a coherent story from the image in the sand tray.

A photograph of the image in the sand tray is a delight for the children and develops a sense of self esteem because an image they have made is considered worth remembering.

10

Play with individuals

It can be helpful to work one to one with children and adults who have special needs, in order to give individual attention, to develop creativity and the capacity to play.

Play is one way to develop communication with people who may find direct talking difficult because they haven't access to words or because they are uncomfortable just talking. It can be safe to play and use play material to share feelings and ideas.

Play is a unique experience in our lives, it has a reality of its own and is a powerful way through which human beings can explore their identities as individuals and in relation to others. Play is the way a child begins to recognise what is 'me' and 'not me' and through play begins to develop a relationship with the world beyond 'me'.

If we consider play to be the central experience for the child to help make sense of the world around her and her place in the world we can explore four basic concepts which will help to structure what and how we play with people with special needs.

Firstly: play is the way children make sense of their world and what is happening to them in that world.

Secondly: play is a developmental process and this determines the complexity of the play but there is much pleasure to be gained from re-enacting early forms of play.

Thirdly: play is a symbolic process where we use objects and ourselves to represent other objects and other selves. Through this symbolic process, the child can experiment with imaginative choices and because it is play and not 'reality' we are appropriately distanced from the consequences of such symbolic choices.

Fourthly: play happens in a special place. When children play they choose their own space for play be it under the table, in a 'den', the bottom of the garden. The child finds a safe place and this is the playing space where our creative life begins.

THE CENTRALITY OF PLAY

Play is a serious and important activity for the child and it is important to recognise this when playing with a child. The adult should play with the child as an equal participant acknowledging the seriousness of the activity for the child. You enter the world of the child and play, but maintain safety and security in the boundaries and rules negotiated before play begins.

PLAY AS A DEVELOPMENTAL PROCESS

Sue Jennings (1990) describes three stages of development in play: embodiment play, projective play and role play.

Embodiment play

Embodiment play is experienced as infant play from birth to about a year old and involves a variety of explorations of the senses. The infant discovers sensation through making sounds and rhythms, makes marks with food and faeces and can imitate. As the child learns to walk, these sensory explorations gain a larger environment and develop accordingly.

Some children who are multiply disabled never move beyond this stage of embodiment play but much can be achieved with an individual child with sounds, touch, taste and imitation.

As the small child explores the world through the senses she begins to explore objects and toys and move towards projective play.

Projective play

The child begins to explore the world of objects and discovers that objects can be used as symbols for something else so a broom becomes a horse and a saucepan a crown.

Role play

As the child develops skill with object play then dramatic play develops through play about the family or places and activities which the child has experienced. Roles then develop and expand from these beginnings.

SYMBOLIC PLAY

Symbolic play is the way the child can explore experiences safely distanced from the reality of their own life. For instance, sexually abused children often play out the power relationships they had with the abuser but through the interactions of puppets so Mr Crocodile becomes the abuser and Miss Mouse the child experiencing the abuse. Through these symbolic interactions children can begin to make sense of what has happened to them but safely distanced from the pain of their direct experience.

Developing symbolic play

The way children play symbolically is also part of a developmental process for the child. When children learn to play with objects they move from simple sequences to more complex play until they can make transformations with objects, changing them to represent something else in play. They integrate this kind of play with role play. This kind of development takes place from about two years of age over about a two year period. This is the time the child learns to play and starts to enjoy make-believe. Once this has been achieved the child is capable of transforming experience in symbolic play.

Garvey (1990) describes the stages as:

1 the child begins to sort out action patterns which are compatible with each object and begins to fit an action to an object, for example, from everything to the mouth to putting a spoon to the mouth;

2 the child combines objects together like cup and saucer;

3 the child sequences actions together like cooking, eating, washing up;

4 the child applies actions to herself, like combing hair, then applies actions to others, like her mother, and then to replicas, like a doll;

5 the child invents appropriate objects which are not present, like pretending to stir coffee without a spoon;

6 the child transforms objects for use in actions; for
   example, she uses a pencil as a spoon to stir imaginary
   coffee in a toy cup.

THE PLAY SPACE

When children play they set the activity apart from 'real' life
by signalling their intention to play and by defining the space
in which they play. When we play with children we need a
space which is safe and has clear boundaries. If there is access
to a play room, this can be the safe place but it must be warm
and comfortable not just an institutionalised playing area
which becomes alienating and unsafe for the child. Play equipment must always be the same material, always available and
this is sometimes not possible in institutional places. Ideally a
play room should contain sand, water, sand trays, a place
where mess can easily be cleared up so that tension about mess
doesn't inhibit play.

   If such a place is not available the adult must create a special
place in which a child feels safe and comfortable. For my work
with children I often play in different buildings so I now use
a blue mat as a safe place. I take this mat around with me.
Placing it down and preparing to play has become part of the
ritual of play sessions. The mat is put down at the beginning
of play and folded at the end of play to signal that the special
time is over.

   I sit on the mat on the floor with the child. The floor is a
safe place so we share it together. This is special time out of
real time, boundaried in space.

MATERIAL FOR PLAY

With my mat I bring a variety of toys and other creative
material which stimulate play. I carry them in large bright bags.
Inside the large bags are a number of white laundry bags which
contain sets of toys. The children can play with any set of toys
they want but only one bag at a time although they can match
toys from different bags so James played with a monster from
the monster bag and a family and a car from the family bag.

   Toys can be collected as you go along. It is quite important
in this kind of work to keep these toys apart from general
play equipment because they become special for children and
if any are lost it is distressing for the child. If this play time

together is special then the toys should also be 'special' to that time and place.

Children are curious to know who else plays with the toys and accept the specialness of our play together and that others play in the same way. When a child wants to keep a toy I explain it is special to other children as well and I find the child has respect for that and a sense of solidarity with the other children. Part of the ground rules for play is that I undertake the responsibility for the toys. I am often asked if I play at home with the toys.

TOYS THAT STIMULATE PLAY

Puppets
Choose puppets which are easy to handle. Glove puppets with large mouths which can be manipulated by the child for biting are very popular. Select puppets which represent those with power and those without to stimulate simple play. Among others, I have a crocodile, a cockerel, a white rabbit and a grey mouse and these are used to express power and lack of power in the children's lives.

Dolls
It is important to have dolls to represent babies with appropriate feeding equipment. It is also important to have dolls to represent the ethnic group to which the child belongs. Dolls with soft bodies are best for storymaking and dramatic family play.

Monsters and heroes
These are important toys for stories developed from the child's experience of TV and books. Small toy figures represent the latest cult heroes or monsters such as ghostbusters, horror monsters, turtles and wrestlers, as well as snakes, witches, spiders, frogs and other objects usually suggested by the child.

This bag of toys is fairly gruesome but perhaps contains the most popular objects for stories and is used by children to explore their own fears and anxieties.

It is important to have heroes both male and female, and villains to stimulate the stories which can be simple or complex according to the ability of the child to play.

SENSORY PLAY

Playdoh, clay, green sticky slime, sticky snakes, worms and other such creatures make stimulating material for sensory play. Just being messy is what many children want to do or making objects and people from soft material and 'scrunching' it up afterwards. Children move from messy play to making objects to storymaking and drama as a natural progression possibly within the course of an hour. Themes are embodied, projected and enacted through the medium of play.

Stage make-up

Stage make-up, in particular aqua-colour, is often used by children as a form of sensory play. Children enjoy the feel of the material, the colour and smell, and the process of touching the colours and making marks on their faces.

If make-up is used in this way I ask children just to imagine they are making a painting on their faces; it does not have to represent anything. They can enjoy the colours and patterns and see what happens. When they have looked at the faces they have made, I ask children to arrange their bodies in a way which goes with the face.

The material offered for play may change according to the child and that person's particular interests. Sometimes older children are afraid of being thought 'childish' if they play with toys so I use drawing materials and stage make-up as we begin. Very soon, as confidence grows and confidentiality is assured, children, adolescents and adults begin to play with and use all the materials.

MAKING A CONTRACT TO PLAY

Once the child and I decide we can play together we discuss how we can make a contract to play together.

The reason for a contract between the two of us is to make rules and boundaries clear from the beginning.

The reason for playing

Firstly we decide why we are playing, what the task will be. Perhaps I might say that we are playing to help you feel good about yourself or we are going to play about why you are living with foster carers. It is important to make the task clear.

I always emphasise the pleasure of play as a way to make sense of experience.

Tell the child how many times you are going to meet, how often and how long each session will last. I tell all children even if they don't have much understanding of time because it still structures the play as an event with a beginning and end in a sequence of time.

If a child is unclear about time, ten minutes before the end I say that we have only time for one more game, or you can choose one more thing out of the bags and then we will have to stop.

RULES OF BEHAVIOUR

I always make clear what behaviour is not acceptable when playing together:

1 no hitting,
2 respect for each other's body,
3 you can say what you like on the mat,
4 you can be rude about people on the mat,
5 off the mat social rules of your home apply,
6 I take responsibility for the toys.

PLAY WITH INDIVIDUALS

When the contract is made and the task defined, then play begins. It is important initially that the child decides what and how to play and chooses the materials for play.

The role of the facilitator is to support the child in play, share in playing if asked by the child, take roles in stories and be the scribe and recorder of all the stories and ideas the child wants recorded.

Some children like their stories taped, others feel constrained by tape but like to hear their stories read. Some children wa' the adult to join in, others don't want the adult to particir but to be audience and sounding board for their ideas.

The facilitator is spectator and supporter of the ch' does not interpret what the child does in play. however, suggest appropriate material for playing ' story or theme and participate by taking roles suggestion. In role she will play the way the but if the suggestions are inappropriate then the facilitator uses the language of children's play and refuses the role saying, 'I'm not playing, it's scary,' or whatever reason is appropriate. The child understands the rule because it is a rule of children's play. The rule applies with adolescents and adults stated in more age appropriate terms.

EXAMPLE: ALAN

Alan, aged 12, was having difficulties coping with his class-mates who teased him and bullied him because he had very limited understanding of social interaction.

At the beginning of our time together he enjoyed drawing and making stories, using the characters from heroes and monsters.

He was angry and helpless about school and at the beginning could see no solutions for himself except some kind of magical solutions. These themes were present in his stories. This is one of his stories:

The Wizard

Once upon a time there was a wizard in a big tower. In one corner he had a steaming cauldron with weird and wonderful smells like ear of newt, mouth of alligator smell, rabbit's blood and many others, some too horrible to name.

On the big black desk in the middle of the room lay his great book of spells which stood almost as large as the caul-dron. His very special wizard's hat and his black magic wand also lay on the desk.

On three shelves at the other end of the room stood many bottles with strange coloured smoke flowing out. By the side of the bottles was a crystal ball and many books of spells, although not as important as the big red one on the desk.

Along the floor were many strange liquids flowing out from the bottom of the cauldron.

There were big cracks in the walls of the tower and out through the window there was another tower where the wicked witch, El Trissta, lived.

Outside were his two black eagles returning home with some news of lost spells and artifacts in the middle of the desert.

The eagles came and told him news of the spell artifacts,

also to tell him the news that the witch was planning to blow up his tower and steal the spell book.

The wizard gathered up his crystal ball, the most important book of his spells, the giant spell book and the wand as well as a few personal possessions and left the tower with his two eagles Shiz and Shaz. He goes to the witch's tower and the witch is making dynamite.

The wizard sent the two eagles to kill the witch and with the dynamite the wizard blew up the witch's tower although he took many artifacts from her spellroom first.

The wizard goes to the desert to find the lost artifacts but is haunted by the ghost of the witch and dies and the books are lost for all time until the late twentieth century when a boy called Alan finds them.

In his story Alan found the spell books but there the story ends because the boy doesn't know how to use them.

There were more stories from Alan, I gave him some help about ways to talk to his peers. He decided that he needed some object to keep in his pocket for difficult moments at school, something he could touch for reassurance. He and his father found a special stone on the beach and Alan kept this in his pocket. Then he worried that he might lose the stone but we decided that in the end that didn't matter because he could always think of the stone and then remember the happy day he had spent with his father when he found it first.

EXAMPLE: JASON

Jason was 8, he had learning difficulties and he lived with his father as his mother had left.

I played with Jason for six sessions to help him express some of his angry feelings and to help his father to understand Jason's need to play.

For the first four sessions Jason played very aggressive stories taking a spider toy as his hero. The themes of these stories and play were about the spider being attacked and because he was horrible and ugly the only thing he could do was attack back.

His next stories were about a group of spiders who lived in a place where there were no mothers because the spiders were so bad that the mothers had left.

As the play developed and Jason gained in self confidence

the character of the spider changed. The spider became a kind creature although at first, though he was kind, he was also starving and nobody would give him food.

In the final play session Jason took two small dolls to represent a father and a son and played a loving relationship with freedom for the son but a home which was safe.

Jason's father watched some of the play and Jason told him about his stories after each session. Father and son began to play more together and the self confidence of both increased. Jason felt safe when he could play with no obligation to achieve but firm rules about behaviour and his concentration increased as he was accepted and what he played was accepted.

STRUCTURED PLAY WITH INDIVIDUALS

It can be useful to use individual play sessions in a structured way to help resolve a particular difficulty.

EXAMPLE: JANET

Janet was 12 and she lived with her mother who sometimes became very drunk so Janet and I used play to develop her self esteem and give her strategies to cope with her situation at home.

We did some play and games about Janet herself and what she looked like, what were her favourite foods, clothes and so on so she began to see herself as being a separate person from her mother, respecting herself and choosing for herself. This helped her to learn that she was not responsible for her mother's drinking.

Our final sessions were about strategies to cope if her mother got drunk; she acted what to say if she needed to get away from the house, how to phone social services or the police. We made a final visit to the police station so she would know the route and where to go rather than just run out of the house and hide in a car park as she had done the last time her mother was out of control. All this was achieved through playing roles, even the visit to the police station was a 'what if'.

At the end of the work Janet felt more in control of herself and her own choices. For many children who are fearful about what they would do in difficult circumstances, an attempt to find solutions in drama which work in reality is very helpful to develop self esteem so they don't feel they are victims of their circumstances.

EXAMPLE: JUNE

June was 8 and had been sexually abused by her uncle. She had learning difficulties but her mum was very supportive and wanted to help June as much as she could.

The play with June was about body boundaries and owner-ship of the body. Her mother was present and reinforced the learning after the play. June's mother had been deprived of play experiences as a young child and she enjoyed watching play and developing ideas to stimulate her daughter's imagi-nation. We played and drew a great deal and made up stories about keeping safe.

We read books together and all the work was reinforced by June's mother who continued to play with her daughter and also to teach other mothers who had difficulties playing with their children.

One year later June is doing well at school and still playing with her mother.

Finally, a little story from Valerie aged 8. She had been neglected and abused as a child but had now found a new family.

EXAMPLE: VALERIE

Once upon a time there was a little girl who was walking with her mother down the street. Then they walked into a little shop.

Soon they found lots of toys to play with.

Soon they bought nearly all the toys in the shop because they were rich.

They bought 90 toys.

Then they went home and went to bed.

The End.

BIBLIOGRAPHICAL SOURCES

Ahlberg, J and A (1989), *Bye Bye Baby*, London: Heinemann

Ahlberg, J and A (1980), *Funnybones*, London: Heinemann

Boal, A (1979), *Theater of the Oppressed*, London: Pluto Press

Boal, A (1995), *The Rainbow of Desire*, London: Routledge

Bowyer, R (1970), *The Lowenfeld World Technique*, Oxford: Pergamon

Bradman, T (1986), *The Bad Babies' Book of Colour*, London: Arrow Books

Bradman, T and Browne, E (1990), *In a Minute*, London: Methuen Children's Books

Carlson, N (1990), *I Like Me*, London: Penguin

Cattanach, A (1992), *Play Therapy with Abused Children*, London: Jessica Kingsley Publishers

Cole, B (1993), *Mummy Laid an Egg*, London: Jonathan Cape

Dominelli, L (1988), *Anti-Racist Social Work*, London: Macmillan Education

Epston, D and White, M (1992), *Experience, Contradiction, Narrative and Imagination: Selected Papers of David Epson and Michael White 1989–1991*, Adelaide: Dulwich Centre Publications

Freeman, L (1982), *It's My Body*, Seattle: Parenting Press

Firth, U (1989), *Autism Explaining the Enigma*, Oxford: Blackwell

Garvey, C (1977, 1990), *Play*, Cambridge, Mass.: Harvard University Press

Harper, A (1988), *What Feels Best*, London: Penguin

Harris, R (1994), *Let's Talk About Sex*, London: Walker Books

Hindman, J (1983), *A Very Touching Book*, Oregon: McClure Hindman Associates

Huizinga, J (1949, reprint 1970), *Homo Ludens*, London: Paladin Books

Hutchins, P (1971), *Titch*, London: Pitman Publishing

Jennings, S (1973), *Remedial Drama*, London: Pitman Publishing

Jennings, S (1986), *Creative Drama in Groupwork*, London: Winslow Press

Jennings, S (1990), *Dramatherapy with Families, Groups and Individuals*, London: Jessica Kingsley Publishers

Jones, T (1981), *Fairy Tales*, London: Penguin

Kliphuis, M (1975), 'Creative Process Therapy', in *Psychotherapy*, vol. 2 (3–4), 283–5

Langer, S (1953), *Feeling and Form*, London: Routledge & Kegan Paul

Lorde, A (1984), *Sister Outsider*, New York: The Crossing Press

McCall Smith, A (1989), *Children of Wax*, Edinburgh: Canongate Publishing

McKee, D (1987), *Not Now, Bernard*, London: Arrow Books

McPhail, D (1988), *Something Special*, London: Penguin

Mayle, P (1973), *Where Did I Come From?*, London: Macmillan

Mazer, A (1990), *The Yellow Button*, London: Bodley Head Children's Books

Peake, A (1989), *My Book, My Body*, London: The Children's Society

Piaget, J (1962), *Play, Dreams and Imitation in Childhood*, London: Routledge & Kegan Paul

Rank, O (1932, reprint 1975), *Art and Artist*, New York: Agathon Press

Rauschenberg, R (1981), 'The Man who turned Life into a Stage Set' by Marina Vaizey, *The Sunday Times*

Rosen, M (1989), *Freckly Feet and Itchy Knees*, London: William Collins

Saphira, M and McIntyre, L (1989), *Look Back, Stride Forward* Auckland, NZ: Papers Inc.

Senn, C (1988), *Vulnerable: Sexual Abuse and People with an Intellectual Handicap*, Downsview, Ontario: G Allen Roeher Institute

Sherborne, V (1990), *Developmental Movement for Children*, Cambridge: Cambridge University Press

Sobsey, D (1994), *Violence and Abuse in the Lives of People with Disabilities*, Baltimore: Paul H Brook

Spolin, V (1986), *Theatre Games for the Classroom*, Evanston, Illinois: Northwestern University Press

Todd, L (1979), *Tortoise, the Trickster*, London: Routledge & Kegan Paul

Vygotsky, L S (1933), 'Play and Its Role in the Mental Development of the Child', in J Bruner, et al (1976), *Play*, London: Penguin

Wells, H G (1911), *Floor Games*, London: Dent

White, M and Epston, D (1989), *Literate Means to Therapeutic Ends*, Adelaide: Dulwich Centre Publications

Wilson, G (1994), *Prowlpuss*, London: Walker Books

Wing, L (1976), 'Problems of Diagnosis and Classification', in L Everard (ed.), *An Approach to Teaching Autistic Children*, Oxford: Pergamon

Yalom, I (1975), *The Theory and Practice of Group Psychotherapy*, New York: Basic Books

APPENDIX

Training for dramatherapists

For those interested in developing therapeutic skills, there are training courses offered by centres approved by the British Association of Dramatherapists.

These centres are:

Institute of Dramatherapy at Roehampton,
Roehampton Institute,
Faculty of Arts & Humanities,
Digby Stuart College,
Roehampton Lane,
London SW15 5PH

University College of Ripon and York St John,
Lord Mayor's Walk,
York Y03 7EX

University of Hertfordshire,
Division of Art & Arts
  Therapies,
Manor Road,
Hatfield,
Herts AL10 9TL

Sesame, Central School of Speech and Drama,
Embassy Theatre,
64 Eton Avenue,
Swiss Cottage,
London NW3 3HY

City College Manchester,
Fielden Centre,
141 Barlow Moor Road,
West Didsbury,
Manchester M20 2PQ

General information

General information about Dramatherapy can be obtained from the professional body for Dramatherapists which is:

British Association for Dramatherapists,
5 Sunnydale Villas,
Durston Road,
Swanage,
Dorset BH19 2HY

Training for play therapy

Training courses in Play Therapy which emphasise the relationship between Play Therapy and Dramatherapy are offered by:

Arts Therapies Secretary,
Roehampton Institute,
Digby Stuart College,
Roehampton Lane,
London SW15 5PH